The Real Ebonics Debate

The Real Ebonics Debate

EDITED BY
**THERESA
PERRY**
AND
**LISA
DELPIT**

*Power,
Language,
and the
Education of
African-American
Children*

Published in
collaboration with
Rethinking Schools

Beacon Press
Boston

Beacon Press
25 Beacon Street
Boston, Massachusetts 02108-2892
www.beacon.org

Beacon Press books
are published under the auspices
of the Unitarian Universalist Association of Congregations.

03   02   01   00   99   98   8   7   6   5   4   3   2   1

Text design by Wesley B.Tanner/Passim Editions
Composition by Wilsted & Taylor Publishing Services

Library of Congress Cataloging-in-Publication Data

The real ebonics debate : power, language, and the education of
     African-American children / edited by Theresa Perry and Lisa Delpit.
          p.   cm.
          "Published in collaboration with Rethinking schools."
          Includes bibliographical references (p.   ).
          ISBN 0-8070-3145-3 (paper : alk. paper)
          1. Afro-Americans—Education.   2. English language—Study and teaching—
     Afro-American students.   3. Black English.   4.Afro-American children—Language.
     5. Language and education—United States.   I. Perry, Theresa.   II. Delpit, Lisa D.
     III. Rethinking schools.
     LC2778.L34R43   1998
     371.829'6073—dc21   97-46828

To Neida Perry
and the late Dan R. Perry,
who raised up and educated
twelve strong, resolute,
and loud-mouthed children,
and to Imani Perry,
that she might continue
in that tradition.

To Maya Delpit,
to the remarkable children
in Carrie Secret's class,
and to all the other brilliant
African-American children
who are destined
to change the world.

Contents

Contents

For six months, the thirty-member African-American task force (school board members, community activists, and teachers) grappled with the underachievement of African-American students enrolled in the Oakland, California, public schools.

The average grade point average for all students in the district was 2.4; for white students it was 2.7; for Asian-American students, 2.4. The average grade point average for African-American students was 1.8. While African Americans made up 53 percent of the student population, they represented 80 percent of suspensions and 71 percent of students labeled as "special needs." Against the backdrop of this dismal picture of school failure, the above-average performance of African-American students at the Prescott Elementary School caught the attention of the task force members.

Prescott Elementary School was the only school in the Oakland school district where the majority of its teachers had voluntarily chosen to participate in the Standard English Proficiency program (SEP). This statewide initiative, begun in 1981, acknowledges the systematic, rule-governed nature of Black English and takes the position that this language should be used to help children learn to read and write in Standard English. On December 21, 1996, the school board unanimously passed the Ebonics resolution, requiring all schools in the district to participate in the Standard English Proficiency program (SEP). This resolution was but one element of a broad strategy developed by the African-American task force, aimed at improving the school performance of African-American students.

The irrational and racist discourse that followed the school board's approval of the Ebonics Resolution has made it almost impossible to have a careful conversation about the important educational, political, and linguistic issues that are embedded in the resolution. *The Real Ebonics Debate: Power, Language, and the Education of African-American Children* provides a much-needed forum for discussion of these issues.

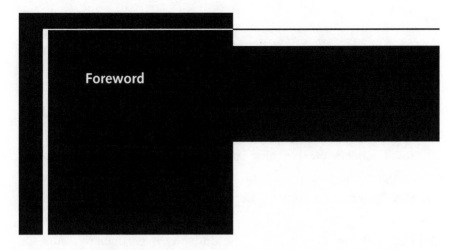

Foreword

Perhaps more than any other debate in education, the study of language grapples with questions of power and identity. We believe it is especially important that African-American educators take the lead in defining the discussion around Ebonics. We are pleased that Theresa Perry and Lisa Delpit approached *Rethinking Schools, An Urban Educational Journal*, with the proposal to guest edit an issue on Ebonics. Both are well-respected educators with long histories of challenging educational practices that are a dis-service to African-American students.

As Lisa Delpit notes in her essay, one cannot be for or against Ebonics. It exists. It is the language many African-American children heard "as their mothers nursed them and changed their diapers and played peek-a-boo with them. It is the language through which they first encountered love, nurturance, and joy."

The national debate on Ebonics did little to clarify the misunderstandings about the history of the language or to help educators develop curriculum. Delpit, Perry, and the other writers in this book offer background history that excavates the race and power dynamics surrounding the development of the language, and discuss how an understanding of Ebonics may affect classroom practice. We believe it is especially important that white educators carefully consider their arguments.

The authors in this book, despite certain differences, have two essential points of unity: a respect for the language spoken by most African-American children — whether one calls that language Ebonics, Black Dialect, or an African-American Language System — and an understanding that African-American children must be taught Standard English if they are to succeed educationally. One of the media's crudest distortions of the Oakland school board's resolution was the mistaken view that Oakland students would be taught Ebonics in place of Standard English.

How teachers view the home language of students and their families plays a significant role in teachers' expectations and respect for students' cultures. Speaking a different dialect or language — whether it is Ebonics, Spanish, or Tagalog — should not prejudice teachers' attitudes toward children. But too often it does. The difficulty is particularly acute for those African-American students who speak Ebonics because many teachers fail to recognize their language as anything other than a substandard form of English. As a result, teachers may view Ebonics-speaking children as stupid or lazy (although these value judgments might be couched in more acceptable terms such as "disadvantaged" or "in need of language remediation").

As the authors in this book point out, Ebonics is not a poor sister to English but a language system with roots in West Africa. It is a language that evolved in struggle and under conditions of extreme oppression — a creative response to a slave society that did its best to erase African language and culture. As the slave masters knew, language is power.

Fundamentally, the controversy that erupted over the Oakland resolution goes beyond linguistics. It is a debate about culture, power, identity, and control. It is a debate about how best to acknowledge and change the reality that our nation's schools are failing African-American students. It is a debate that will never end until our society and our schools provide true access and opportunity to African Americans.

The Real Ebonics Debate began as a special issue of the journal *Rethinking Schools*. For the first time in the history of the magazine, guest editors solicited and wrote the articles and oversaw editorial content from the inception to implementation. We hope this special book will help generate a discussion about Black Language that is, in the words of Theresa Perry, "as complex, sophisticated, and nuanced as the language itself."

— Editors of *Rethinking Schools*

1   Introductions

We die. That may be the meaning of life. But we do language. That may be the measure of our lives.

Toni Morrison
Address on receipt of the 1993 Nobel Prize for Literature

"I 'on Know Why They Be Trippin'": Reflections on the Ebonics Debate

THERESA PERRY

To say that African-American children were not achieving in the Oakland public schools would have been an understatement. Comprising 53 percent of the students enrolled in the only predominantly Black school district in the state of California, African-American children accounted for 80 percent of the school system's suspensions and 71 percent of students classified as having special needs. Their average grade point average was a D+.

These stark, painful realities, reflective of the Oakland school system's inability to ensure even a modicum of academic success for African-American children, are what motivated the school board to unanimously approve the Black Language/Ebonics resolution. Essentially, this resolution maintained that Black Language/Ebonics was a legitimate, rule-based, systematic language, and that this language was the primary language of many African-American children enrolled in the Oakland school system. The board further maintained that Ebonics, the home/community language of African-American children, should not be stigmatized, and that this language should be affirmed, maintained, and used to help African-American children acquire fluency in the standard code.

Understanding that most teachers have little, if any, accurate knowledge about Black Language and are likely to harbor negative attitudes about the language and its speakers, primarily because of their sociopolitical location, and understanding also the relationship of literacy skills to school achievement, the resolution called for the implementation of an educational program for the district's teachers that would focus on the

3

nature and history of Black Language/Ebonics. The assumption was that such a program would address the teachers' knowledge gap about Black Language, begin the process of changing their attitudes about the language, and help teachers figure out how to use the rich and varied linguistic abilities of African-American children to help them become fluent readers and writers.

Despite what some might consider "distracting noises" in the resolution's initial formulation, and despite the resolution's early and sustained misrepresentation in the media, this was the essence and the intent of the board's resolution. The resolution called for the same intervention that had been mandated in the historic 1978 *Martin Luther King, Jr. v. Ann Arbor School Board* case, the Black English case. Separated by almost two decades, representing different geographic regions and school districts with vastly different racial/ethnic demographics, the circumstances surrounding the school lives of African-American children in Ann Arbor, Michigan, in 1978, and in Oakland, California, in 1997 — circumstances that motivated both the Ann Arbor case and the Oakland resolution — were strikingly similar. Sixty-six percent of the plaintiff children in the Ann Arbor case had been classified as special needs. In this liberal, affluent college town, African Americans were also overrepresented in the number of suspensions and underrepresented in honors classes. In the predominantly white school district of Ann Arbor and in the minority/majority district of Oakland, the caste positionality of African Americans was the same. So much for the promise of multiculturalism.[1]

MEDIA MISREPRESENTATIONS

With few exceptions, mainstream media[2] presented the Oakland resolution as a decision by the school board to abandon the teaching of Standard English and in its stead to teach Black Language/Ebonics. Not only was this not the intent of the resolution, this is not what was contained in the original resolution (see The Oakland Ebonics Resolution, page 143). Whether in response to the Oakland resolution and/or the media's misrepresentation of the resolution, with little or no awareness of their orchestrated movements, editorial writers, columnists, pundits, talk show hosts, educational leaders, and spokespeople for the race (for Black people) formed a coalition of individuals who together took aim at the Oakland resolution. Black and white, members of the religious right, liberal Democrats, neoconservatives, staunch conservatives, left liberals, and the privileged — such was the reach of this unintentional coalition of individuals that, in the weeks and months after the passage of the Oakland resolution, vigorously registered their opposition to it.

The right-wing talk show hosts had a field day. The Internet hummed. Called lunatics, Afrocentrists, accused of giving up on Black kids, and of legitimizing slang — these were just some of the invectives hurled at the members of the Oakland school board. What was so disorienting for some African Americans, regardless of how they understood the board's resolution or their position on it, was this strange configuration of folks who were attacking African-American educators and community activists who obviously care deeply about the welfare of African-American children. How is it that long-time civil rights organizations and activists ended up on the same side of the barricade with their traditional and current adversaries? How did it happen that Jesse Jackson, Kwesi Mfume, and Maya Angelou joined with William Bennett, George Will, Rush Limbaugh, and Pete Wilson to take aim at the Oakland decision? Why did folks who love the language, use it exquisitely, and whose personal and political power is in no small measure tied to their use of Black Language, register ambivalence or outright rejection of the board's call for the recognition of the legitimacy of Black Language and its suggestion that it be used to help African-American children become fluent readers and writers?

It is, of course, easy to blame the media for creating these strange bedfellows.

The media deserve blame for their gross misrepresentation of the resolution and their failure to capture the resolution's essential elements. Even after the spokespeople for the Oakland school board, the superintendent, and members of the school board had asserted over and over again that the school system was not abandoning the teaching of Standard English, TV news accounts continued to lead with this claim. Reporters continued to ask Black spokespeople what they thought about the Oakland decision to teach Ebonics. One had to search long and hard in the print media for the full text of the board's resolution. Instead, one found phrases, sentences taken out of context, and outright distortions of the original resolution.

AFRICAN-AMERICAN RESPONSE

It is also easy, as I initially did, to blame African Americans for internalized racism, for colonized consciousness. Early on, while trying to make sense of this strange configuration of allies, to interpret the remarks of Jesse Jackson, Maya Angelou, and other Black talking heads, I offered my analysis: "Black Language is the last uncontested arena of Black shame," I argued. "We have let go of a good deal of the shame attached to Black hair. Not that it is all gone. Black soap opera and singing stars as well as Black academics now proudly sport dreads, braids, Afros, natural hair styles. Black Language is largely an uncontested arena of Black shame." The media's misrepresentation of the case, as well as the sense of shame some African Americans have about the use of certain varieties of Black Language in certain contexts, may have contributed to this strange configuration of allies. These variables alone, however, cannot explain why so many African Americans were tentative, ambivalent, or even downright opposed to the Oakland resolution.

At the close of the twentieth century, Africans Americans have become quite adept at reading the media, its text, and subtext. We did not need anybody to tell us what the O. J. Simpson case was really about. We read its coded meanings. In spite of the mainstream media's hegemonic narrative, we knew the narrative surrounding the case and its aftermath was not simply or primarily about O. J. Simpson, a batterer, who in a jealous rage allegedly murdered his wife and her suspected lover. We didn't even need clarity about the person of O. J. Simpson to deconstruct the narrative. We didn't have to erase from our consciousness the knowledge of O. J.'s tenuous relationship to the Black community and to Black women before we would distrust the police and the criminal justice system. The brother on the corner, the college professor, the high school student, the abused wife read the media's narrative about the case and its submerged meaning long before Toni Morrison registered her assessment:

> The official story has thrown Mr. Simpson into that representative role. He is not an individual who underwent and was acquitted from a murder trial. He has become the whole race needing correction, incarceration, censoring, silencing; the race that needs its civil rights disassembled; the race that is sign and symbol of domestic violence; the race that has made trial by jury a luxury rather than a right and placed affirmative action legislation in even greater jeopardy. This is the consequence and function of official stories: to impose the will of a dominant culture (Morrison, 1997, p. xxviii).

Why were we as a people able to read the O. J. Simpson case but not the Black Language/Ebonics resolution? Why were so many African Americans unable to get to the core of the resolution, to read against the hegemonic narrative? It is indeed curious that so many African Americans missed the point — even if you consider the media's misrepresentation of the case and our ambivalencies about the use of certain varieties of Black Language in a given context.

What, in contrast, is there about our material condition in America in relationship to the criminal justice system that has produced such shared consciousness about the Simpson case? How does this relationship contrast with the relationship of African Americans to the public school system in the post–civil rights era?

In one week, in late November 1996, I encountered or heard about four African-American males who were involved with the criminal justice system. On Monday, a colleague, a faculty member at a well-known university, canceled our five o'clock appointment. He had to be in court with his 16-year-old son; it was his son's third court appearance on charges that were all eventually dropped. On Tuesday, in the midst of my work with a young African-American man on his college applications, this young man, quite abruptly, stood up and told me he had to leave to go with his family to visit an older brother who was in jail. On Wednesday, while speaking with another colleague on the telephone, he asked me if I had heard the news. Bracing myself, he told me that his two sons had been arrested over the weekend. Later that same week, my daughter told me about an African-American friend of hers, a law student, who, when he goes to record stores, walks fast, up and down the aisles, to disorient the clerks who are following him.

Indeed, one in four Black men — and virtually all Black families via relatives and extended family members — are involved with the criminal justice system. The courts, the criminal justice system, surveillance have become part of the collective consciousness of African Americans. Our stance towards the criminal justice system, our shared consciousness, has been influenced by these material realities, consolidated by national, galvanizing events such as the Rodney King case.

VARIETY OF FACTORS

Indeed, many factors contributed to the unpredictable, confused, and confusing alliances of African Americans in reaction to the Oakland resolution. Not the least of these is the existence of a dominant, powerful conversation about schooling that is shaped by white businessmen, white reformers, and white scholars and is predicated on "generic solutions to broken schools." At the same time, there is the absence of a public counternarrative about the education of African Americans, framed by African Americans themselves and predicated on an acknowledgment of our continuing position as a historically oppressed people. There has always been a dominant narrative about public education and the education of African Americans. However, in the post–civil rights era, perhaps for the first time in history, African American scholars, educators, and political activists have not shaped a public counterconversation with contested and uncontested domains. Furthermore, while race significantly affects the school lives of virtually all African-American children, the way that this occurs varies, depending on the school's demographics and geographic location and the child's social position. This variation (a few children acquire a high level of skills, some acquire minimal skills, and some none; the racist violence perpetrated against children is subtle in some schools, overt in others), as well as the absence of a public discourse about race and achievement, effectively camouflages the oppressive force of school in contemporary Black life, thus militating against the formation of a collective consciousness.

In my estimation, too many African Americans sided with our traditional adversaries in attacking the Oakland resolution because of the hegemonic character of the national discourse about education and the corresponding absence of a counterconversation led by African Americans — a counterconversation that refuses to disconnect discussions of education from our sociopolitical position in the larger society, our cultural formations, our position as a racial caste group.

The way the Ebonics case was coded in TV news accounts also played an important role in generating negative reactions from African Americans. As TV commentators and reporters talked about the resolution, the image that was projected over and over again was that of a Black male speaking Black slang in a school context. Besides equating Black Language with slang, TV news accounts presented the image of Black students speaking this informal variety of Black Language in a school context. It is important to note that the church and the school are both formal institutional settings in the African-American community. To say that school was a formal institution for African Americans is not to imply that children at no time were allowed to speak their home/community language. It is to say that school was conceptualized as a place where children were expected to work on, practice, and demonstrate competency in Standard English. It is to acknowledge that in these schools there were speech acts, routines, and rituals, when a student was expected to perform in Standard English, as well as occasions when they were not because this expectation would have constrained teaching and learning.

A friend of mine, who loves Black Language in all of its varieties — vernacular, literary, and standard — was adamant that while the "shame explanation" could account for some of the negative reactions of African Americans to the Oakland resolution, it did not capture the complexities embedded in the response of African Americans. On more than one occasion, he said, "I don't know, Theresa. They (the media) are not talking about what we are talking about when they say 'Black Language.'" As I spoke with him and with other African Americans, I began to understand that his ambivalence about the Oakland resolution was rooted in concern about the narrow definition of Black Language being represented in the media in discussions and commentaries about the Oakland resolution, and his fear that this would be the understanding of Black Language that the public would be left with. As I spoke with other African Americans who were also ambivalent about the Oakland resolution, and for whom it would have been a stretch for me to say that their ambivalence was primarily attributable to their shame about our language, I began to understand that besides being bothered by the equation of Black Language with one of its most informal varieties, these individuals were also concerned about the implication that Black Language doesn't have multiple varieties, oral and written, formal and informal, vernacular and literary, as well as the excision from the public conversation of the notion that for African Americans, language use is fundamentally and exquisitely contextual.

A community leader and scholar weighed in on the Oakland resolution when she heard that I was working on a special issue of *Rethinking Schools* on Black Language/Ebonics. Without strong feelings, in a calm, centered manner, she recalled how her deceased father, a Black college president, in the evenings would read to her the dialect poetry of Paul Laurence Dunbar, commenting on its beauty. She went on to note that in her community and family, it was expected that you would have fluency in and see the beauty, power, and possibilities in the formal and informal registers of Black Language (the language of the blues, the narrative of Frederick Douglass, the poetry of Langston Hughes, the sermons of James Weldon Johnson and Howard Thurman). It was also expected that you would have fluency in the so-called white Standard English.

MISREPRESENTING EBONICS

What I came to understand is that many factors contributed to the negative reaction of many African Americans to the Oakland resolution. These include TV images representing Black Language/Ebonics as the equivalent of Black slang, the positioning of Black children speaking this variety in school (which is perceived by African Americans as a formal environment), and the media's framing and coding of the case in a way that was antithetical to the notion that language use is contextual (almost a truism of African Americans). For many African Americans, this resolution stood in opposition to their historic stance of wanting their children to gain oral and written competence in the formal and informal varieties of Black Language and "white" Standard English. And thus the Oakland resolution, contrary to its enormous possibilities, threatened to be another instance of the narrowing of options for African-American children.

There were other African Americans who strongly supported the Oakland resolution and yet equivocated, wondering if this was a conversation that African Americans could have productively in public. Instinctively, they knew that the Oakland resolution would precipitate a national conversation about race, specifically about the mental and moral capacities of Black people. They were right. White Americans had a field day. On TV programs, in the halls of Congress, and on the infamous talk shows circuit, white Americans made pronouncements: African Americans were too stupid to learn the language. The media's fictive and stereotypic version of Black Language became the butt of jokes. White person after white person opined that if others could learn the language, why couldn't African Americans? U.S. Education Secretary Richard Riley called Black Language a "nonstandard form of English." President Clinton termed it slang. State and federal legislators drafted legislation to prevent federal and state moneys from being used on any educational program based on Black Language. The quintessential liberal columnist Ellen Goodman registered her outrage. To her, Black Language was nothing but a "second-class language for a second-class life." She was more than exercised by the thought that the Oakland school board had made "'I be' the equivalent of 'Je suis.'"

While I fully understood that in America any conversation about African Americans always threatens to careen out of control, to become a coded and sometimes not-so-coded conversation about race, I applauded and continue to applaud the courageous stance of the Oakland school board and their steadfastness in the face of the force and reach of the opposition.

And for a moment I was naively hopeful that despite the opposition and the racist discourse about the resolution, the resolution would also generate a discussion about Black Language that would be as complex, sophisticated, and nuanced as the language itself. This was not to be. Where were the essays, op-ed pieces, magazine stories, or panel discussions that systematically laid open the power, beauty, complexities, and pedagogical possibilities embedded in Black Language? With anxious anticipation, I waited for just one careful conversation in the mainstream media about the power African Americans attach to the spoken word, and how this power is necessarily linked to an understanding (cognitively, emotionally, and socially) of audience and context. Did not the late Malcolm X remind us of this when, as he committed himself to copying the entire dictionary, memorizing the meaning of the words he did not know, he said that he wanted to be as articulate in his communication with the late Elijah Muhammed as he had been when he was working the streets as a hustler? None of the talking heads bothered to make a connection between Black Language/Ebonics and the way rhythm, rhyme, metaphor, repetition are and were used by Jesse Jackson, Martin Luther King, Jr., Rev. William Borders, and African-American preachers all over this country. None bothered to explore the relationship between Toni Morrison's use of the call and response sequence in her award-winning novel, *Beloved*, or the artistic use of the Black vernacular forms by Alice Walker, Gwendolyn Brooks, Zora Neale Hurston, and the Oakland resolution, which instructed the superintendent to "implement the best possible academic program for imparting instruction to African-American students in their primary language *for the combined purposes of maintaining the legitimacy and richness of such language . . . and to facilitate the acquisition and mastery of English language skills.*" (Emphasis added.)

WHAT WASN'T SAID

Indeed, in trying to understand the reactions to the Oakland resolution, what was not said — the conversations that did not occur, the topics left unexplored, the voices not heard — is as important as what was said.

No one interviewed or talked to even a handful of those tens of thousands of African Americans who grew up speaking Black Language as their home and community language and who have became fluent in the standard code. Nobody thought it worthwhile to try and find out about those "best practices," the rituals, routines, and practices institutionalized in historically Black schools, churches, and communities that helped Black Language speakers become fluent readers, writers, and powerful speakers. If they had, they would have heard stories similar to one Oprah recalled on the air (interestingly, not in response to the Black Language/Ebonics debate), about how, when she was growing up, she knew by heart every one of the sermons from James Weldon Johnson's *God's Trombone*, and must have performed them all in every church in her hometown.

They would have heard stories similar in theme if not in detail to that of Skip Griffin (a leader of the Black Student Movement at Harvard College in the late 1960s and early 1970s and currently director of community affairs at the *Boston Globe*), about how he and his buddies, for whom life outside school was always more interesting than life inside, became motivated to become learned. According to him, their experience of the power of the word, that is, how teachers and preachers were able to use the word, to instruct, to inspire hope, to comfort, to expose social injustices, and to mobilize people into a movement, made them want to become educated. About his decision to become a committed student, he said, "I wanted to get me some big words." This sentiment is strikingly similar to that expressed by Richard Lischer in his discussion of Martin Luther King's self-consciousness about his development as a preacher (1995) and by Malcolm X himself. For Malcolm X, it was Bimbi, a fellow prisoner and the first person he met for whom words were power, who motivated him to want to become literate.

They would have heard the stories similar to those of bell hooks, Marva Perry, Nancy Hughes,[3] about how as children and adolescents they worked diligently, throughout the year, with their Sunday school teachers on presentations for the many seasonal programs, constitutive of Black church life in the pre-civil rights era; how, after these presentations had been made to Sunday school classes and had met the required standard of excellence, they would be performed for the entire church. We would have heard about the corpus of Freedom Speeches from the African-American, American, and European traditions that were routinely performed at school assemblies and in local, regional, and national oratorical contests; how these speeches were read, reread, analyzed, memorized; about the many hours spent preparing to deliver these speeches, to interpret them such that they would capture the writer's intent and speak to the African-American community.

Perhaps the most significant omission in discussions about Black Language/Ebonics in the aftermath of the Oakland resolution, particularly if what is at issue is African-American school achievement, was the failure to examine the meaning and function of the literacy acts — speaking, reading, and writing — in the African-American community: the failure to see these literacy acts as distinct, interconnected, and interdependent moments that are most powerful when they function for freedom, for racial uplift, leadership, citizenship (Anderson, 1988; Cornelius, 1991; Gates, 1991; Perry, 1996; Shaw, 1996; Steptoe, 1979).

HOW WHITENESS FUNCTIONS

In the aftermath of the Oakland resolution, the silence of white school reformers, white progressive educators, and their organizations was deafening. These individuals and organizations did not lead or follow the lead of the Linguistic Society of America and issue statements in support of the Oakland resolution. Their avowed understandings about the role of prior knowledge in teaching and learning, about the importance of meeting students where they are, about antiracist multicultural education, about "whiteness" — none of these understandings were seemingly compelling enough to motivate them or their organizations to publicly enter the debate.

It underconceptualizes what occurred to simply label the discourse of the mainstream media about the Oakland resolution as racist. The media's reaction to the Oakland resolution provides us with a powerful, contemporary example of how whiteness functions in the American society. The social historian David Roediger (1991) defines whiteness as that complex admixture of longing and hate that white people have for African Americans, their cultural formations, and their cultural products. White America, particularly the educated elite, embrace African American writers — Toni Morrison, Alice Walker, Gwendolyn Brooks, Maya Angelou. August Wilson was awarded two Pulitzer Prizes for *Fences* and *The Piano Lesson*. Liberals and left liberals may still remember Jesse Jackson's moving speech at the 1988 Democratic national convention, framed by the formulaic Black refrain, "they catch the early bus." College and university campuses around this country can't get enough of Cornel West. White Americans are attracted to, embrace, at least superficially, African Americans who would not be the kind of writers, dramatists, or scholars they are if they were not rooted in and operating out of African-American linguistic traditions. And at the same time, these same opinion makers are repulsed by the people, by Black people, their language, their aesthetics, their rhythms, their history, that is represented, symbolized, interpreted in the African-American literary and scholarly traditions and commodified in popular culture.

No, Black Language/Ebonics is not merely a pass-through language, only to be used to get to Standard English. The members of the Oakland school board had it right in their initial resolution when they affirmed the importance of fluency in Black Language and Standard English. They knew that fluency in the standard code can never be the singular goal if, and this is a big if, our schools are to participate in the creation of the next generation of African-American scholars, preachers, dramatists, writers, blues men and women — African-American leaders.

I will submit that one of the reasons [Ebonics] is a problem, if you will — a controversy — is that you cannot divorce language from its speakers. And if you have a people who have been disenfranchised, are neglected, are rejected, it is very difficult for the society at large to elevate their language. And, thus, when you start to try to make a case with legitimizing Ebonics — a way of communicating by some, although not all African-Americans speak it — you, in effect, are talking about legitimizing a group of people. You are talking about bringing them to a status comparable to society at large. And that's always a difficult proposition. So, in a certain sense, we cannot talk about Ebonics separate and distinct from the state of African-American people in the United States as a neglected and as an underclass, marginalized, if you will, people.

Orlando Taylor

Professor of Communications at Howard University

Emerge *magazine, April 1997*

What Should Teachers Do?
Ebonics and Culturally Responsive Instruction

LISA
DELPIT

The "Ebonics Debate" has created much more heat than light for most of the country. For teachers trying to determine what implications there might be for classroom practice, enlightenment has been a completely nonexistent commodity. I have been asked often enough recently, "What do you think about Ebonics? Are you for it or against it?" My answer must be neither. I can be neither for Ebonics or against Ebonics any more than I can be for or against air. It exists. It is the language spoken by many of our African-American children. It is the language they heard as their mothers nursed them and changed their diapers and played peek-a-boo with them. It is the language through which they first encountered love, nurturance, and joy.

On the other hand, most teachers of those African-American children who have been least well-served by educational systems believe that their students' life chances will be further hampered if they do not learn Standard English. In the stratified society in which we live, they are absolutely correct. While having access to the politically mandated language form will not, by any means, guarantee economic success (witness the growing numbers of unemployed African Americans holding doctorates), not having access will almost certainly guarantee failure.

So what must teachers do? Should they spend their time relentlessly "correcting" their Ebonics-speaking children's language so that it might conform to what we have learned to refer to as Standard English? Despite good intentions, constant correction seldom has the desired effect. Such correction increases cognitive monitoring of speech, thereby making talking difficult. To illustrate, I have frequently taught a relatively simple new "dialect" to classes of preservice teachers. In this dialect, the phonetic element "iz" is added after the first consonant or consonant cluster in each syllable of a word. (*Maybe* becomes miz-ay-biz-ee and *apple*, iz-ap-piz-le.) After a bit of drill and practice, the students are asked to tell a partner in "iz" language why they decided to become teachers. Most only haltingly attempt a few words before lapsing into either silence or into Standard English. During a follow-up discussion, all students invariably speak of the impossibility of attempting to apply rules while trying to formulate and express a thought. Forcing speakers to monitor their language typically produces silence.

Correction may also affect students' attitudes toward their teachers. In a recent research project, middle school, inner-city students were interviewed about their attitudes toward their teachers and school. One young woman complained bitterly, "Mrs. ———— always be interrupting to make you 'talk correct' and stuff. She be butting into your conversations when you not even talking to her! She need to mind her own business." Clearly this student will be unlikely to either follow the teacher's directives or to want to imitate her speech style.

GROUP IDENTITY

Issues of group identity may also affect students' oral production of a different dialect. Researcher Sharon Nelson-Barber (1982), in a study of phonologic aspects of Pima Indian language, found that, in grades 1–3, the children's English most approximated the standard dialect of their teachers. But surprisingly, by fourth grade, when one might assume growing competence in standard forms, their language moved significantly toward the local dialect. These fourth graders had the *competence* to express themselves in a more standard form but chose, consciously or unconsciously, to use the language of those in their local environments. The researcher believes that, by ages eight to nine, these children became aware of their group membership and its importance to their well-being, and this realization was reflected in their language. They may also have become increasingly aware of the schools's negative attitude toward their community and found it necessary — through choice of linguistic form — to decide with which camp to identify.

What should teachers do about helping students acquire an additional oral form? First, they should recognize that the linguistic form a student brings to school is intimately connected with loved ones, community, and personal identity. To suggest that this form is "wrong" or, even worse, ignorant, is to suggest that something is wrong with the student and his or her family. To denigrate your language is, then, in African-American terms, to "talk about your mama." Anyone who knows anything about African-American culture knows the consequences of that speech act!

On the other hand, it is equally important to understand that students who do not have access to the politically popular dialect form in this country are less likely to succeed economically than their peers who do. How can both realities be embraced in classroom instruction?

It is possible and desirable to make the actual study of language diversity a part of the curriculum for all students. For younger children, discussions about the differences in the ways TV characters from different cultural groups speak can provide a starting point. A collection of the many children's books written in the dialects of various cultural groups can also provide a wonderful basis for learning about linguistic diversity,[1] as can audiotaped stories narrated by individuals from different cultures, including taped books read by members of the children's home communities. Mrs. Pat, a teacher chronicled by Stanford University researcher Shirley Brice Heath (1983), had her students become language "detectives," interviewing a variety of individuals and listening to the radio and TV to discover the differences and similarities in the ways people talked. Children can learn that there are many ways of saying the same thing, and that certain contexts suggest particular kinds of linguistic performances.

Some teachers have groups of students create bilingual dictionaries of their own language form and Standard English. Both the students and the teacher become engaged in identifying terms and deciding upon the best translations. This can be done as generational dictionaries, too, given the proliferation of "youth culture" terms growing out of the Ebonics-influenced tendency for the continual regeneration of vocabulary. Contrastive grammatical structures can be studied similarly, but, of course, as the Oakland policy suggests, teachers must be aware of the grammatical structure of Ebonics before they can launch into this complex study.

Other teachers have had students become involved with standard forms through various kinds of role-play. For example, memorizing parts for drama productions allow students to practice and "get the feel" of speaking Standard English while not under the threat of correction. A master teacher of African-American children in Oakland, Carrie Secret, uses this technique and extends it so that students videotape their practice performances and self-critique them as to the appropriate use of Standard English (see interview with Carrie Secret, page 79). (But I must add that Carrie's use of drama and oration goes much beyond acquiring Standard English. She inspires pride and community connections that are truly wondrous to behold.) The use of self-critique of recorded forms may prove even more useful than I initially realized. California State University—Hayward professor Etta Hollins has reported that just by leaving a tape recorder on during an informal class period and playing it back with no comment, students began to code-switch — moving between Standard English and Ebonics — more effectively. It appears that they may have not realized which language form they were using until they heard themselves speak on tape.

Young students can create puppet shows or role-play cartoon characters — many "superheroes" speak almost hypercorrect standard English! Playing a role eliminates the possibility of implying that the child's language is inadequate and suggests, instead, that different language forms are appropriate in different contexts. Some other teachers in New York City have had their students produce a news show every day for the rest of the school. The students take on the personae of famous newscasters, keeping in character as they develop and read their news reports. Discussions ensue about whether Tom Brokaw would have said it that way, again taking the focus off the child's speech.

Although most educators think of Black Language as primarily differing in grammar and syntax, there are other differences in oral language of which teachers should be aware in a multicultural context, particularly in discourse style and language use. Harvard University researcher Sarah Michaels and other researchers identified differences in children's narratives at "sharing time" (Michaels & Cazden, 1986). They found that there was a tendency among young white children to tell "topic-centered" narratives — stories focused on one event — and a tendency among Black youngsters, especially girls, to tell "episodic" narratives — stories that include shifting scenes and are typically longer. While these differences are interesting in themselves, what is of greater significance is adults' responses to the differences. C. B. Cazden (1988) reports on a subsequent project in which a white adult was taped reading the oral narratives of Black and white first graders, with all syntax dialectal markers removed. Adults were asked to listen to the stories and comment about the children's likelihood of success in school. The researchers were surprised by the differential responses given by Black and white adults.

VARYING REACTIONS

In responding to the retelling of a Black child's story, the white adults were uniformly negative, making such comments as "terrible story, incoherent" and "[n]ot a story at all in the sense of describing something that happened." Asked to judge this child's academic competence, all of the white adults rated her below the children who told "topic-centered" stories. Most of these adults also predicted difficulties for this child's future school career, such as "This child might have trouble reading," that she exhibited "language problems that affect school achievement," and that "family problems" or "emotional problems" might hamper her academic progress.

The Black adults had very different reactions. They found this child's story "well formed, easy to understand, and interesting, with lots of detail and description." Even though all five of these adults mentioned the "shifts" and "associations" or "nonlinear" quality of the story, they did not find these features distracting. Three of the Black adults selected the story as the best of the five they had heard, and all but one judged the child as exceptionally bright, highly verbal, and successful in school (Cazden, 1988).

This is not a story about racism, but one about cultural familiarity. However, when differences in narrative style produce differences in interpretation of competence, the pedagogical implications are evident. If children who produce stories based on differing discourse styles are expected to have trouble reading and viewed as having language, family, or emotional problems, as was the case with the informants quoted by Cazden, they are unlikely to be viewed as ready for the same challenging instruction awarded students whose language patterns more closely parallel the teacher's.

Most teachers are particularly concerned about how speaking Ebonics might affect learning to read. There is little evidence that speaking another mutually intelligible language form, per se, negatively affects one's ability to learn to read (Sim, 1982). For commonsensical proof, one need only reflect on nonstandard English-speaking Africans who, though enslaved, not only taught themselves to read English, but did so under threat of severe punishment or death. But children who speak Ebonics do have a more difficult time becoming proficient readers. Why? In part, appropriate instructional methodologies are frequently not adopted. There is ample evidence that children who do not come to school with knowledge about letters, sounds, and symbols need to experience some explicit instruction in these areas in order to become independent readers (see Mary Rhodes Hoover, page 71). Another explanation is that, where teachers' assessments of competence are influenced by the language children speak, teachers may develop low expectations for certain students and subsequently teach them less (Sims, 1982). A third explanation rests in teachers' confusing the teaching of reading with the teaching of a new language form.

Reading researcher Patricia Cunningham (1976–1997) found that teachers across the United States were more likely to correct reading miscues that were "dialect"-related ("Here go a table" for "Here is a table") than those that were "nondialect"-related ("Here is a dog" for "There is a dog"). Seventy-eight percent of the former types of miscues were corrected, compared with only 27 percent of the latter. She concludes that the teachers were acting out of ignorance, not realizing that "here go" and "here is" represent the same meaning in some Black children's language.

In my observations of many classrooms, however, I have come to conclude that even when teachers recognize the similarity of meaning, they are likely to correct Ebonics-related miscues. Consider a typical example:

TEXT: Yesterday I washed my brother's clothes.

STUDENT'S RENDITION: Yesterday I wash my bruvver close.

The subsequent exchange between student and teacher sounds something like this:

T: Wait, let's go back. What's that word again? [Points at *washed*.]

S: Wash.

T: No. Look at it again. What letters do you see at the end? You see "e-d." Do you remember what we say when we see those letters on the end of the word?

S: "ed."

T: OK, but in this case we say washed. Can you say that?

S: Wash*ed*.

T: Good. Now read it again.

S: Yesterday I wash*ed* my bruvver . . .

T: Wait a minute, what's that word again? [Points to *brother*.]

S: Bruvver.

T: No. Look at these letters in the middle. [Points to brother.] Remember to read what you see. Do you remember how we say that sound? Put your tongue between your teeth and say /th/. . . .

The lesson continues in such a fashion, the teacher proceeding to correct the student's Ebonics-influenced pronunciations and grammar while ignoring that fact that the student had to have comprehended the sentence in order to translate it into her own language. Such instruction occurs daily and blocks reading development in a number of ways. First, because children become better readers by having the opportunity to read, the overcorrection exhibited in this lesson means that this child will be less likely to become a fluent reader than other children that are not interrupted so consistently. Second, a complete focus on code and pronunciation blocks children's understanding that reading is essentially a meaning-making process. This child, who understands the text, is led to believe that she is doing something wrong. She is encouraged to think of reading not as something you do to get a message, but something you pronounce. Third, constant corrections by the teacher are likely to cause this student and others like her to resist reading and to resent the teacher.

Language researcher Robert Berdan (1980) reports that, after observing the kind of teaching routine described above in a number of settings, he incorporated the teacher behaviors into a reading instruction exercise that he used with students in a college class. He put together sundry rules from a number of American social and regional dialects to create what he called the "language of Atlantis." Students were then called upon to read aloud in this dialect they did not know. When they made errors he interrupted them, using some of the same statements and comments he had heard elementary school teachers routinely make to their students. He concludes:

> The results were rather shocking. By the time these Ph.D Candidates in English or linguistics had read 10–20 words, I could make them sound totally illiterate. . . . The first thing that goes is sentence intonation: they sound like they are reading a list from the telephone book. Comment on their pronunciation a bit more, and they begin to subvocalize, rehearsing pronunciations for themselves before they dare to say them out loud. They begin to guess at pronunciations. . . .

They switch letters around for no reason. They stumble; they repeat. In short, when I attack them for their failure to conform to my demands for Atlantis English pronunciations, they sound very much like the worst of the second graders in any of the classrooms I have observed.

They also begin to fidget. They wad up their papers, bite their fingernails, whisper, and some finally refuse to continue. They do all the things that children do while they are busily failing to learn to read.

The moral of this story is not to confuse learning a new language form with reading comprehension. To do so will only confuse the child, leading her away from those intuitive understandings about language that will promote reading development and toward a school career of resistance and a lifetime of avoiding reading.

Unlike unplanned oral language or public reading, writing lends itself to editing. While conversational talk is spontaneous and must be responsive to an immediate context, writing is a mediated process that may be written and rewritten any number of times before being introduced to public scrutiny. Consequently, writing is more amenable to rule application — one may first write freely to get one's thoughts down, and then edit to hone the message and apply specific spelling, syntactical, or punctuation rules. My college students who had such difficulty talking in the "iz" dialect found writing it, with the rules displayed before them, a relatively easy task.

To conclude, the teacher's job is to provide access to the national "standard" as well as to understand the language the children speak sufficiently to celebrate its beauty. The verbal adroitness, the cogent and quick wit, the brilliant use of metaphor, the facility in rhythm and rhyme, evident in the language of Jesse Jackson, Whoopi Goldberg, Toni Morrison, Henry Louis Gates, Jr., Tupac Shakur, and Maya Angelou, as well as in that of many inner-city Black students, may all be drawn upon to facilitate school learning. The teacher must know how to effectively teach reading and writing to students whose culture and language differ from that of the school, and must understand how and why students decide to add another language form to their repertoire. All we can do is provide students with access to additional language forms. Inevitably, each speaker will make his or her own decision about what to say in any context.

But I must end with a caveat that we keep in mind a simple truth: Despite our necessary efforts to provide access to Standard English, such access will not make any of our students more intelligent. It will not teach them math or science or geography — or, for that matter, compassion, courage, or responsibility. Let us not become so overly concerned with the language form that we ignore academic and moral content. Access to the standard language may be necessary, but it is definitely not sufficient to produce intelligent, competent caretakers of the future.

2 What Is Ebonics?

Official language smitheried to sanction ignorance and preserve privilege is a suit of armor, polished to shocking glitter, a husk from which the knight departed long ago. Yet there it is; dumb, predatory, sentimental. Exciting reverence in schoolchildren, providing shelter for despots, summoning false memories of stability, harmony among the public.

Toni Morrison
Address on receipt of the 1993 Nobel Prize for Literature

Black English/Ebonics: What It Be Like?

**GENEVA
SMITHERMAN**

*I looked at my hands, they looked new
I looked at my feet, and they did too
I got a new way of walkin, and a new way
of talkin.*

Traditional Black Gospel Song

The month after the Oakland school board passed its resolution, the term *Ebonics* turned twenty-four years old. Yeah, dass right, the name is over two decades old. It was coined by a group of Black scholars as a new way of talkin bout the language of African slave descendants. Like the message of that old Gospel tune, "Ebonics" was about transformation, about intellectuals among the Talented Tenth striking a blow for the linguistic liberation of our people. The guru in this group of scholars at that "Language and the Urban Child" conference, convened in St. Louis, Missouri, in January 1973, was the brilliant clinical psychologist, Dr. Robert L. Williams, now Professor Emeritus, Washington University. In the book of conference proceedings Williams published in 1975, he captures the thinking of that historical moment:

> A significant incident occurred at the conference. The black conferees were so critical of the work on the subject done by white researchers, many of whom also happened to be present, that they decided to caucus among themselves and define black language from a black perspective. It was in this caucus that the term *Ebonics* was created. [The term refers to] linguistic and paralinguistic features which on a concentric continuum represent the communicative competence of the West African, Caribbean, and United States slave descendant of African origin. It includes the various idioms, patois, argots,

29

ideolects, and social dialects of black people, especially those who have been forced to adapt to colonial circumstances. (1975, Preface, Introduction)

For this group of scholars, the conceptual framework of "Ebonics" represented an avenue for decolonization of the African-American mind, a way to begin repairing the psycholinguistically maimed psyche of Blacks in America. As Paulo Freire (1985) would put it twelve years later, "language variations (female language, ethnic language, dialects) are intimately interconnected with, coincide with, and express identity. They help defend one's sense of identity and they are absolutely necessary in the process of struggling for liberation" (p. 186). Ebonics reaffirms the interrelatedness of language and culture and links Africans in America with Africans around the globe.

Ebonics: neither "broken" English, nor "sloppy" speech, nor merely "slang," nor some bizarre lingo spoken only by baggy-pants-wearing Black kids. Rather, the variety of Ebonics spoken in the United States (hereafter USEB) is rooted in the Black American Oral Tradition and represents a synthesis of African (primarily West African) and European (primarily English) linguistic-cultural traditions. The linguistic shape of the words in USEB can readily be identified as Standard English, that is, the Language of Wider Communication here in the United States (hereafter LWC), but these words do not always have the same meaning in USEB as in LWC. Further, there are many words of direct African origin — for example, *okay, gorilla, cola, jazz* — that are now part of LWC (often without props to us African slave descendants). However, what gives Black Language (un-huh, dat ain no typo, I meant "language") its distinctiveness is the nuanced meanings of these English words, the pronunciations, the ways in which the words are combined to form grammatical statements, and the communicative practices of the USEB-speaking community. In short, USEB may be thought of as the Africanization of American English.

PATTERNS OF EBONICS

In the next section, I discuss the following patterns of USEB: (1) aspectual *be*; (2) stressed *been*; (3) multiple negation; (4) adjacency/context in possessives; (5) postvocalic /r/ deletion; (6) copula absence; (7) camouflaged and other unique lexical forms.

Consider this statement, which comes from some Black women just kickin it in the beauty shop (gloss: conversational chit-chat at a hair salon): "The Brotha be lookin good; that's what got the Sista nose open!" In this statement, *Brotha* is USEB for an African-American man, *lookin good* refers to his style, his attractive appearance (not necessarily the same thing as physical beauty in USEB), *Sista* is USEB for an African-American woman, and her passionate love for the Brotha is conveyed by the phrase *nose open* (in USEB, the kind of passionate love that makes you vulnerable to exploitation). *Sista nose* is standard USEB grammar for denoting possession, indicated by adjacency/context (that is, rather than the LWC /'s, s'/). The use of *be* means that the quality of *lookin good* is not limited to the present moment but reflects the Brotha's past, present, and future essence. As in the case of Efik and other Niger-Congo languages, USEB has an aspectual verb system, conveyed by the use of the English verb *be* to denote iterativity (that is, a recurring or habitual state-of-affairs; contrast *He be lookin good* with *He lookin good*, which refers to the present moment only — not the kind of *lookin good* that opens the nose!). Note further that many Black writers and Rap artists employ the spellings "Brotha" and "Sista." Now, they ain just tryin to be cute. These orthographic representations are used to convey a phonological pattern derived from the influence of West African languages, many of which do not have an /r/ sound. Also in these language communities, kinship terms may be used when referring to African people, whether biologically related or not.

Of course there is overlap between USEB and colloquial, everyday American English — for example, use of "ain't," ending sentences with prepositions, double negatives. However, there are critical distinctions that separate linguistically competent USEB speakers from the wanna-bes. For example, the colloquial speaker says *gonna* or *goin to* for the LWC form *going to*. But the USEB speaker uses the nasalized vowel form, producing a sound close to, but not identical with, LWC *gone*, thus: "What she go (n) do now?," that is, in LWC, "What is she going to do now?" Another example is in negation patterns. While those obsessed with the "national mania for correctness" often rail against colloquial speakers' double negatives, USEB is distinctive not only for its negative inversion, but also for its *multiple* negatives, that is, three or more negatives formed from combinations of indefinite pronouns and/or adjectives. Check out this exclamation of complex negative inversion from a devout churchgoer: "Don't nobody don't know God can't tell me nothin!," that is, in LWC, "A person who doesn't believe in God and isn't saved has no credibility with me."

As mentioned above, USEB words may look like mainstream American English, but the usage and meaning are different. This is the source of a good deal of miscommunication and misunderstanding between USEB and LWC speakers. In response to the question, "Is she married?," the USEB speaker may answer "She been married." If the speaker pronounces *been* without stress, it means the woman in question was once married but is now divorced. If the speaker pronounces *been* with stress, it means she married a long time ago and is still married. Another example is the use of LWC words that are "camouflaged" (Spears, 1982). For example, in the USEB statement, "She come tellin me I'n [didn't] know what I was talkin bout," the verb *come* does not denote motion as in LWC. Rather the meaning of *come* in this context is one of indignation, that is, in LWC, "She had the audacity to tell me that I didn't know what I was talking about. How dare she!" Yet another kind of cross communication example comes from semantic inversion. Due to crossover and the popular appeal of Michael Jackson, most people are aware that *bad* in USEB translates to *good* in LWC; however, lexical items that haven't enjoyed such a high degree of crossover are problematic in these crosscultural exchanges. For example, consider the following form of address common among many

Black males: "Yo, Dog!" *Dog* is a linguistic symbol of male bonding, most likely derived from the African-American fraternity tradition of referring to pledges as *dogs*. *Yo, Dog!* was used by a Brotha on lock down (gloss: imprisoned) to address his European-American male psychiatrist as an expression of camaraderie. Turns out, though, that this white psychiatrist was not yet down (gloss: hip, understanding of the Black Cultural framework). He misinterpreted the Brotha's greeting and made an issue of the "insult."

The above are only some of the patterns in the grammatical, phonological, and semantic systems of USEB. To explore the full 360 degrees of USEB, we need to move on to styles of speaking. In fact, it is the area of communicative practices — rhetorical strategies and modes of discourse — that cuts across gender, generation, and class in the African-American community. USEB speech acts may be classified as follows: (1) Call-Response; (2) Tonal Semantics; (3) Narrativizing; (4) Proverb Use/Proverbializing; (5) Signification/Signifyin; (6) The Dozens/Snappin/Joanin. Discussion of two of these discourse modes follows.

Signification or, more commonly, *signifyin*, which can be rendered with or without the phonological and morphosyntactical patterns of USEB, is a form of ritualized insult in which a speaker puts down, talks about, needles — signifies on — other speakers. In this communicative practice, the speaker deploys exaggeration, irony, and indirection as a way of saying something on two different levels at once. It is often used to send a message of social critique, a bit of social commentary on the actions or statements of someone who is in need of a wake-up call. When signifyin is done with verbal dexterity, it avoids the creation of social distance between speaker and audience because the rich humor makes you laugh to keep from crying. Like Malcolm X who once began a speech with these words: "Mr. Moderator, Brother Lomax, Brothas and Sistas, friends and enemies." Now, you don't usually begin a speech by addressing your enemies. Thus, Malcolm's signifyin statement let his audience know that he knew inimical forces were in their midst. Or like one of the deacons at this Traditional Black Church, where the preacher would never deal with the problems and issues folk were facing on a daily basis. Rather, he was always preachin bout the pearly gates and how great thangs was gon be at dat home up in the sky. So one day this deacon said to the preacher, "Reb, you know, I got a home in Heaven, but I ain't homesick!"

Signifyin is engaged in by all age groups and by both males and females in the Black community. It has the following characteristics: (1) indirection, circumlocution; (2) metaphorical-imagistic (images rooted in the everyday real world); (3) humorous, ironic; (4) rhythmic fluency; (5) teachy, but not preachy; (6) directed at person(s) present in the speech situation (signifiers do not talk behind your back); (7) punning, play on words; (8) introduction of the semantically or logically unexpected.

TYPES OF SIGNIFICATION

There are two types of Signification. One type is leveled at a person's mother (and occasionally at other relatives). Traditionally, this first type was referred to as "The Dozens"/"playin The Dozens." The second type of signifyin is aimed at a person, action, or thing, either just for fun or for corrective criticism. Today, the two types of Signification are being conflated under a more general form of discourse, referred to as "snappin."

To fully appreciate the skill and complexity of Signification, we shall analyze in some detail a conversational excerpt involving two Sistas in a group of several at a wedding shower:

> LINDA: Girl, what up with that head? [Referring to her friend's hairstyle.]
>
> BETTY: Ask yo momma. [Laughter from all the Sistas on this conversational set.]
>
> LINDA: Oh, so you going there, huh? Well, I *DID* ask my momma. And she said, "Cain't you see that Betty look like her momma spit her out?" [Laughter from all, including Betty.]

Betty and Linda signify on each other. Instead of answering Linda's question directly, Betty decides to inform Linda that the condition of her hairstyle is none of Linda's business by responding with "Ask yo momma." The usual expectation in a conversation is that a speaker's question will be answered honestly and sincerely; thus Betty's unexpected indirection produces laughter from the listeners.

Speech act theory indicates that communication succeeds or fails as a result of the illocutionary (that is, intended) and perlocutionary (that is, received) effects of a message. The surface meaning of "yo momma" for those outside the USEB speech community is simply "your mother/mom." However, within the Black speech community, the utterance immediately signals that an insult has been hurled. The intended and received meaning of *yo momma* is invective; the game of ritual insult begins with participants creating the most appropriate, humorous, spontaneous, creative, exaggerated/untrue retorts that they can come up with.

The source of the retort "Ask yo momma" probably stems from family patterns in which mothers are consulted ("asked") about all kinds of things, great or small. Fathers may even respond to their children's questions or requests by saying "Ask your mother." In USEB, the speaker does not intend the direct meaning, "You should go and ask your mother about this situation." Rather, given the conversational context, the speaker is indirectly saying "Let the game of The Dozens begin." Linda clearly recognizes the entry into this game as indicated by her response, "Oh, so you going there, huh?" Unskilled players, lacking a spontaneous, apposite, humorous retort, would have let the conversation end at this point. However, Linda shows adeptness in playing the game. She regroups momentarily ("Oh, so you going there, huh?") and fires back skillfully. In fact, she "caps" (gloss: wins) this exchange with a more clever retort. Although Betty's use of the intragroup expression, *ask yo momma*, is humorous and sets up a challenge, it is formulaic, simplistic, and stylized. In this instance, it cannot, and does not, beat: "Well, I *DID* ask my momma. And she said, 'Cain't you see that Betty look like her momma spit her out?'" (Troutman-Robinson and Smitherman, 1997).

Although Rev. Jesse Jackson and Sista Maya Angelou came out in the national news and dissed the Oakland school board's resolution, they are well versed in USEB. Twenty years ago, in my first major work on USEB, *Talkin and Testifyin*, I quoted both at length and lauded them as linguistic role models, who are adept at capitalizing on the forms of Black Language to convey profound political messages. Like Jesse who is down wit Signification: "Pimp, punk, prostitute, preacher, Ph.D. — all the P's, you still in slavery!" Thus he conveys the message that all members of the African-American community, regardless of their social status, are marginalized and disempowered, by virtue of U.S. historically institutionalized racism and skin color bias. (Jesse also uses copula absence here — "you still in slavery" — which has not been found in any of the dialects of British English that came over on the *Mayflower*, but which is used widely in the languages of West Africa.)

THE DOZENS

As mentioned above, The Dozens is one of several significant speech acts in USEB. This ritualized game of insult has analogues in West African communicative practices (see Smitherman, 1995, and the several references cited there). Also referred to as "snappin" by many members of the Hip Hop Nation, The Dozens is like "Yo momma so dumb she thought a quarterback was a refund!"

Sista Maya Angelou is so bad she don't play The Dozens, she play The Thirteens! She uses this USEB discourse mode to critique the actions of Blacks and whites. Here how she do it:

> (The Thirteens Black):
> Your Momma took to shouting
> Your Poppa's gone to war,
> Your sister's in the streets
> Your brother's in the bar,
> The thirteens. Right On . . .
> And you, you make me sorry
> You out here by yourself,
> I'd call you something dirty,
> But there just ain't nothing left,
> cept
> The thirteens. Right On . . .

(The Thirteens White):
Your daughter wears a jock strap,
Your son he wears a bra
Your brother jonesed your cousin
in the back seat of the car.
The thirteens. Right On . . .
Your money thinks you're something
But if I'd learned to curse,
I'd tell you what your name is
But there just ain't nothing worse
than
The thirteens. Right On.

(Angelou, 1971)

African-French psychiatrist Frantz Fanon (1967) taught that "every dialect, every language, is a way of thinking. To speak means to assume a culture." To speak Ebonics is to assume the cultural legacy of U.S. slave descendants of African origin. To speak Ebonics is to assert the power of this tradition in the quest to resolve the unfinished business of being African in America. While years of massive research (done in the 1960s and early 1970s) on the language of this group (mostly by white scholars) did indeed debunk cognitive-linguistic deficiency theory, in its place arose social inadequacy theory. Although the language was shown to be systematic and rule-governed, since it is not accepted by the white mainstream, difference became deficit all over again, and in the process, Africans in America suffered further dislocation. To speak (of/on/about) Ebonics, to consciously employ this terminology and conceptual framework, as those Black scholars did back in 1973, and as the Oakland school board has done a generation later, is to be bout the business of relocating African Americans to subject position. Large and in charge, as the Hip Hoppers say, Ebonics, then and now, symbolizes a new way of talkin the walk about language and liberatory education for African Americans.

The immediate and continuing media response to the Oakland resolution has been, overwhelmingly, one of mockery, ridicule, and outrage. Notice, for example, the common charge that the Oakland resolution is an attempt to elevate "street slang" to the level of Shakespeare, say. This is, of course, a clever but willful category error: Every group has its slang (defined as "the nonstandard vocabulary of a given culture") — even the media, not to mention the Elizabethans, as a cursory reading of the footnotes to Shakespeare's plays and poems quickly reveals.

In the media's brief moments of lucidity, however, linguists (among other specialists) have been invited to the media's party and asked to shed light on what they imagine to be technical or scientific questions. The two that I address below are the most prevalent in my experience:

LANGUAGE AND GENETICS

First question: How can the victims of specious arguments about genetic difference (with respect to IQ, for example) support the notion "that African Language Systems are genetically based"?

Among linguists, Ebonics is commonly known as Black English or African-American English (AAE — the term used below), names not used in the resolution for ideological reasons: to establish that AAE is a language distinct from English.

As is clear from the resolution, but not from the severely cropped passages of it that the media and the politicians chose to highlight, the claim is that AAE has characteristics that derive from the languages that enslaved peoples brought with them from West Africa, a widely held though not uncontroversial claim among linguists. Consider the language of the resolution:

> WHEREAS, these [scholarly] studies have also demonstrated that African Language Systems are genetically based and not a dialect of English; and
>
> WHEREAS, these studies demonstrate that such West and Niger-Congo African languages have been officially recognized and addressed in the mainstream public educational community as worth of study, understanding, or application of its principles, laws and structures for the benefit of African-American students both in terms of positive appreciation of the language and these students' acquisition and mastery of English language skills. . . .

The intent of the first clause is clarified in the slightly revised version of the resolution to:

> WHEREAS, these [scholarly] studies have also demonstrated that African Language Systems have origins in West [African] and Niger-Congo languages and are not merely dialects of English. . . .

The metaphorical use of terms from biology is common in historical linguistics; there is nothing unusual about their use, and certainly nothing biological or genetic about it, except for the obvious fact that it is human beings — creatures of biology — who are moving languages along and in their separate directions. Thus we speak, for example, of the genetic relationship that exists between English and German: that there is a reconstructed "ancestor" language (Proto West Germanic, in this case) from which the "daughter" languages English and German, among other "daughters," are both descended. In a somewhat different way, the claim goes, AAE is historically derived from certain West African languages as well as from English. West African grammatical structures are superficially masked by English words: a creole account of the origins of AAE.

AAE is thus not in the genes of African Americans, for an Asian-American child growing up in a linguistic environment in which AAE is spoken naturally grows to be an AAE-speaking person — a common enough occurrence in Oakland, I would imagine. Since the capacity for language is part of their genetic endowment, all infants raised under normal conditions learn the language(s) of their environment. But they are not predisposed toward any specific language by the socially constructed categories of race or class, nor is this the claim of the Oakland resolution.

LANGUAGE AND DIALECT

Second question: Is AAE a "legitimate" language or "merely" a dialect of some "legitimate" language (a question of concern to Rep. Peter T. King (R-NY), who quickly introduced a House resolution denying federal funds to "any program that is based upon the premise that AAE is a legitimate language")?

Behind this question lies the assumption that the technical terms *language* and *dialect* can, in the context of such modifiers as *legitimate* and *merely*, be used to answer the question. But, though the term "language" is used in linguistics, there it stipulatively defines the thing-in-nature that linguists seek to understand: a highly idealized state of the human mind/ brain that holds of an individual when we say that she or he has a language — an internal or "I-language," in the sense of Noam Chomsky. That is, the linguist wants to know what is in the mind (ultimately, in the brain) of a person when we say that she or he knows a language, not what's out there in the air or on paper — the external (or E-) language that common sense understandably but mistakenly directs our attention to. Thus, the linguist's term *language* is like the terms *momentum* or *force* in physics, whose stipulated meanings are quite different from those of ordinary language, in the same way that the concepts of science are far removed from folk psychology. For example, linguists take for granted notions that abstract severely away from reality, like "the ideal speaker-listener in a completely homogeneous speech-community," in the same way that physicists take for granted notions like "frictionless planes" — conditions that do not and could not hold of nature, though our acceptance of them in science appears to lead us toward a partial explanation of nature.

Our commonsense understanding of the term *language* is quite different, of course; so from this point of view there are languages out there ("E[xternal]-languages") that we feel confident in naming: American Sign Language, Chinese, French, Haitian Creole, Malayalam, Navajo, Swahili, Yoruba, and so on; and there is a commonsense test for whether a way of speaking or signing is different from or the same as some other way of speaking or signing, a test based on mutual intelligibility: If we can sign or talk to one another, then we have the same language; if we can't, then we don't. It's that simple.

We assume further that there are standard versions of these languages, the pinnacles that each dialect speaker is supposed to aspire to, but that which normally — for reasons of class, or race, or geography — she or he is not able to reach. On this view, dialects are diminished varieties of a standard ("legitimate") language, a value judgment that has no standing in linguistics. For, on the scientific point of view, all (I-) languages are rule-governed systems of equal complexity and interest — instantiations of the capacity for language that each infant enters the world with.

A second commonsense definition of language, central to this discussion, lies in the quip that a language is a dialect with an army and a navy — or a school system. This definition suggests, correctly, that languages are defined politically not scientifically. For example, Swedish and Norwegian, though mutually intelligible, are counted as different languages (in contradiction with the common-sense test) simply because a political boundary divides Sweden from Norway, while Cantonese, Fujianese, Mandarin, and so on, though not mutually intelligible, are considered to be dialects of Chinese because they are historically related, typologically alike, and located within the national boundary of the People's Republic of China.

On this definition, then, AAE is clearly a language since — though lacking an army or a navy — it does have one school system, or at least its school board, solidly behind it. Thus, a way of speaking becomes a language by declaration — as is usually the case: A way of speaking is a language if you say it is. It is a legitimate language if it has the force of community consensus behind it — a school board resolution, say.

WHY THE OUTRAGE

A third question: Why the outrage over the resolution in the media and among politicians?

In my own view it has to do with the fact that in the United States — as in many parts of the industrialized world — language prejudice remains a "legitimate" prejudice; that is, one can generally say the most appalling things about people's speech without fear of correction or contradiction. The exercise of this prejudice in the United States is often, but not only, a shield for racism, thus allowing the holders of racist views a freedom no longer readily acceptable in civil society. Let a Fuzzy Zoeller deal with Tiger Woods in an overtly racist manner and he must immediately apologize, drop out of a major golf tournament, and lose his K-Mart endorsements. This is not the case for anyone reviling African Americans in general for their language. This, and its thinly veiled racism, you can continue to get away with as, for example, an examination of many of the more than 3,000 Ebonics Web sites on the Internet quickly reveals.

Couple this freedom to express language prejudice with the fact that the Oakland resolution was promulgated by and in a community of color and the outrage is predictable. For the resolution provides a convenient excuse for politicians and the media to lower themselves once again to an occasion.

It is this language prejudice and its expression rather than the Oakland resolution that ought to be the object of our outrage and our attention. And in part it is toward the eradication of this prejudice that the resolution is directed. For this and for the other sound educational reasons raised in the resolution, the Oakland school board is to be strongly supported.

On June 7, 1997, I participated in a panel discussion at the National Association of Black Journalists (NABJ, Region 1) meeting in Boston. The panel was formed around a question, so let me pose (and answer) it as the fourth question in this series. However, since answering this fourth question requires nothing of linguistics, but merely the ability to read and analyze the newspapers carefully, I have set it off here in what might be considered a commentary and a guide.

"Ebonics: Did we [the media] do the story justice?"

The short answer: Hardly any.

The details follow, though here I deal only with the print media. Others will have to assess radio and TV, for I have had no time to follow them. However, my impression from talking to those who did and from transcripts sent to me is that there the story was treated with much the same disdain and incompetence. For example, on *Fox News Sunday* (December 22, 1996), Tucker Carlson — asked for his reaction to a gross misrepresentation of the Oakland resolution — responded as follows, with great ignorance and little style:

> Well, I think it sounds like something the Klan thought up. I mean, this is — you know, it's like saying "OK, don't speak intelligible En-English. You'll never get a job." I mean, this is — this is a language where nobody knows how to conjugate the verbs. I mean, it's ridiculous. . . .

Returning now to the claim that the print media did little justice to the Ebonics story: First of all, it is important to point out that it is often the early coverage that counts. Once the story is gotten wrong, there is little that can be done; for after the wrong story, quickly follow the talk show and op-ed page artists, whose role appears to be to drive spikes into graves. Informed, balanced stories then generally come too far after the fact, and letters of clarification to the editor — always balanced by contrary letters — are not given the credibility lavished on real, live newspersons. Such was the course more or less followed by the print media on the Oakland resolution.

First there was some simple and brief reportage, in the *Boston Globe* of December 20, 1996, for example (A3): "A California city's schools stand behind black English," quickly followed by more culturally correct views, editorial denunciation, and columnal outrage. Thus on December 23, 1996 (also in the *Boston Globe* [B1]) — in a column partly written in AAE, "Ebonics ain't proper answer," the syndicated columnist Patricia Smith opposed the resolution with a version of the argument now widely used against bilingual education:

> We learned because we have the capacity to learn, so how can we say that our children don't possess that same capacity? . . . As Black kids, we were introduced to a world we had to enter in order to survive, and then we were offered the tools to get there. What they're saying in Oakland is that those kids are too dumb to learn the way we did, and that's insulting.

She struggled and won, so why make life any easier for the students of today? But not everyone won; in fact, relatively few did. Moreover, it's no longer Smith's imperfectly remembered mythic Golden Age — if there ever was one, for as Benjamin Franklin observed, "The Golden Age never was the present age" (Poor Richard['s Almanack] Improved 1750). And in Oakland the fact is that 71 percent of the students in special education are African Americans, who also make up 64 percent of the students held back each year — in a 96 percent people-of-color school system (African American, Asian American, and Latino). Quite obviously, since so many of these students can't be academic failures, it must be that they are not being offered the tools. Thus there should be Smith's "panic in the air. . . . The answer? Ebonics!" Perhaps — if by *Ebonics* is meant the educational measures that the Oakland school board has in mind. For clearly, Oakland needs to do whatever in its wisdom it deems necessary even if it offends the sensibilities of an outraged columnist and her romanticization of the past.

So it goes with the syndicated columns, whose titles often give some of the flavor of the attack: William Raspberry's uninformed characterization of AAE: "no right or wrong expressions, no consistent spellings or pronunciations and no discernible rules" (*Washington Post*, December 26,

1996); Ellen Goodman's "A 'Language' for a Second-Class Life" (*Boston Globe*, December 27, 1996); Mary McGrory accusing the Oakland board of "legitimizing gibberish."

On the *New York Times* editorial page, an enraged Brent Staples makes an early Afrocentrism charge — one of many that will follow ("The Trap of Ethnic Identity: How Africa Came to Oakland," Editorial Notebook, January 4, 1997), raising in a later editorial the fear that the resolution will "drive out the middle-class families that keep schools and other city institutions afloat" [with "their mainstream values and ideas"] (Editorial Notebook, January 24, 1997). Obviously, the middle class is the savior of us all. Frank Rich, also in the *New York Times* ("The Ebonic Plague," January 8, 1997) observed, "There isn't a public personage of stature in the land, white or Black, left or right, Democrat or Republican, who doesn't say that the Oakland, Calif., school board was wrong . . . ." So don't be bold enough to draw your own conclusions in the face of all this political posturing.

Mike Royko (*Chicago Tribune*, January 8, 1997) carried on as expected: "Some momma, she writes me and ax why I don't write no column in Ebonics. I tell the hoe that be wack because I don't know how to talk Ebonics," as did Shelby Steele ("Indoctrination Isn't Teaching," *New York Times*, January 10, 1997) and Jeff Jacoby ("Ebonics: The Self-Esteem Movement Goes Off the Deep End," *Boston Globe*, January 23, 1997), with Jacoby's confusions between the status of immigrant English and AAE and his unhelpful, invidious comparisons between American Jews and African Americans.

A SAD RECORD

A sad, accusatory record, all in all. There were some exceptions, of course. For example, very early on the *Boston Globe* ran a fairly balanced editorial ("English Lessons in Oakland," December 21, 1996), which, however, was undone by its subsequent barrage of op-ed commentary. And the *New York Times* ran an excellent op-ed piece by Patricia J. Williams ("The Hidden Meanings of 'Black English,'" December 29, 1996). Margo Jefferson, in her [cultural] Critic's Notebook "The 2 Faces of Ebonics: Disguise and

Giveaway" (January 7, 1997), wrote, "It is easy to dismiss the subject [Ebonics] with glib gibes or to enshrine it in sentimental bombast. It's hard work to start making sense of all the contradictions." She then proceeded to take on the hard work of sorting through the contradictions.

Other exceptions to the hard-hitting syndicated columns and editorials came in the form of an occasional story written by someone who bothered to talk to persons (linguists and educators) who might be presumed to know something about the issues; that is by a reporter who approached it the way one might approach an issue about the economy or medicine. E.g., Pamela Burdman's "Ebonics Tests Linguistic Definition; Politics, Tempers Rule, Scholars Say" (*San Francisco Chronicle*, December 26, 1996, A1), and Jeremy Pawloski's "Mass. Legislator Files Bill Barring Ebonics" (*Bay State Banner*, January 9, 1997, at1).

As for the left liberal press — weeklies generally: It has the habit of collapsing in the face of tough cultural issues involving, as this one does, race and class. For example, *The Nation* gave its editorial space on the issue over to A. J. Verdelle ("Classroom Rap," January 2, 1997), the author of *The Good Negress* — a novel that celebrates the advantages of learning "the King's English." Verdelle's view of the resolution is very little different from Patricia Smith's:

> The pedagogical strategy advanced by ebonics adds unnecessary steps to our children's already complicated path toward learning, a path obstructed in most cases by the widespread belief and unrelenting message that African-Americans lack intelligence — a position that ebonics seems, unwittingly, to support. . . . To name African-American misstatement as a kind of pseudo-phonics is to legitimize it, to bronze it. Couldn't we just as accurately call it classroom rap? . . . Quite frankly, the Oakland strategy seems to be pedagogy run amok. (Ebonics: gone nuts, looking foolish.)

And Louis Menand in *The New Yorker*'s weekly "Comment" ("Johnny Be Good: Ebonics and the Language of Cultural Separatism," January 13, 1997), concludes that "subcultures flourish when they are just part of life, not part of the curriculum. When they acquire official patronage, they're on the way to the museum." Menand seems not to understand that there is nothing "sub" about AAE in Oakland.

The in-depth stories came later, too much later: Rene Sanchez's "Ebonics — Without the Emotion" (*Washington Post National Weekly Edition*, January 13, 1997); Peter Applebome's "Dispute Over Ebonics Reflects a Volatile Mix That Roils Urban Education" (*New York Times*, March 1, 1997, at 10); and others. These are the kind of thoughtful, daunting, densely packed stories that occupy whole pages and that readers set aside to read later only to find that they have disappeared into the recycling bin. They are too late and too much, especially for readers who have heard it all already.

GETTING IT RIGHT

The NABJ panel ended on a fifth question: How to do things better?

My simple advice:

1. Do the story right the first time, for that is often the only time there is. It is not generally the case that a story appears in a fallow news season the way the Ebonics story did, giving the media so many chances to get the story right, or seriously wrong.

2. Talk to people who might know something about the issues, the way you would when dealing with an issue about the economy.

3. Realize that in education, there is very little of importance that is without a history and politics. Ebonics, by other names, has been with us for a very long time. And it is not going to go away any time soon.

There is also advice for persons who get contacted on such matters: Be willing to spend a lot of time with reporters or to make them spend time with you. For example, I talked for an hour with a *San Francisco Chronicle* reporter and offered more time if she needed it. I tried to make sure she got the story right, and she did. Of course, that doesn't necessarily work; I also spent a lot of time with a freelance writer who turned out to be preparing an article for the right libertarian journal *Liberty*. He didn't get it right, but then, he didn't want to.

I know that it is not the English language that hurts me, but what the oppressors do with it, how they shape it to become a territory that limits and defines, how they make it a weapon that can shame, humiliate, colonize.

bell hooks
Teaching to Transgress

In the study of language in school, pupils were made to scoff at the Negro dialect as some peculiar possession of the Negro which they should despise, rather than directed to study the background of this language as a broken-down African tongue — in short to understand their own linguistic history. . . .

Carter Godwin Woodson
from The Mis-Education of the Negro

What Is Black English? What Is Ebonics?

ERNIE SMITH

The features of the language of African Americans — U.S. slave descendants of West and Niger-Congo African origin — have been recognized, described, and discussed for decades. While in recent years the appellations *Vernacular Black English*, *Black Vernacular English*, *Black English Vernacular*, and *African American Vernacular English* have gained some popularity, the phrase most prevalently used is *Black English.*

In the 1970s and 1980s, several books appeared on the language of slave descendants of African origin with *Black English* as their title. These include *Black English: Its History and Usage in the United States*, by Joseph Dillard (1972); *Black American English: Its Background and Its Usage in the Schools and in Literature*, edited by Paul Stoller (1975); *Black English: A Seminar*, edited by Deborah Sears Harrison and Tom Trabasso (1976); *Black English: Educational Equity and the Law*, edited by John Chambers Jr. (1983).

Conspicuously, in none of these works is "Black English" defined. By using the word *English*, these works inherently posit that the language of African Americans is "English." And they also tacitly postulate that, being a variant of English, there is a genetic kinship between the language of African Americans with the Germanic language family to which English belongs. Yet, from a historical linguistic perspective, in terms of the "base" from which the grammatical features of "Black English" derive, nothing could be further from the truth. As a number of scholars have argued since the 1930s, African-American speech is an African Language System — the linguistic continuation of Africa in Black America.

WHAT IS "BLACK ENGLISH"?

In an attempt to find empirical data supporting the view that the language of African Americans is a dialect of English, I searched the literature on "Black English." Although I found ample debate on whether "Black English" emerged as a result of a pidgin/creole hybridization process or as a result of African slaves being taught Old English "baby talk," I found no empirical evidence that English is even the "base" from which "Black English" derives. This brings us to the issue of what criteria are used for defining and classifying any language, including English, in terms of its "genetic" or familial kinship.

In the *American Heritage Dictionary*, the word *English* is defined, in part, as "the West Germanic language of the English (people) divided historically into Old English, Middle English, and Modern English and now spoken in the British Isles, the United States and numerous other countries." While the definition tells us that English is a West Germanic language, the question remains: By what criteria was it discerned and decided that English is related to or akin to German and belongs to the West Germanic family of the Indo-European languages? Was it based on grammar rules, vocabulary, historical origins, or what?

According to Leonard R. Palmer in his text *Descriptive and Comparative Linguistics: A Critical Introduction* (1978), to establish a kinship or "relationship" between languages, one must go beyond vocabulary and look at grammar:

> For . . . words are often borrowed by one language from another as a result of cultural contact. . . . What constitutes the most certain evidence of relationship is resemblance of grammatical structure, for languages retain their native structure even after their vocabularies have been swamped by foreign borrowing, such as has been the case for English. . . . (p. 23)

This prompts the question: What precisely is meant by the words *grammar* or *grammatical structure*? In their text *Contemporary Linguis-*

tics: An Introduction (1993) W. O'Grady, M. Dobrovosky, and M. Arnoff state:

> In investigating linguistic competence, linguists focus on the mental system that allows human beings to form and interpret the words and sentences of their language. This system is called a grammar. . . . One of the fundamental claims of modern linguistic analysis is that all languages have a grammar. This can be verified by considering a few simple facts. Since all languages are spoken, they must have phonetic and phonological systems; since they all have words and sentences, they also must have a morphology and a syntax; and since these words and sentences have systematic meanings, there obviously must be semantic principles as well. As these are the very things that make up a grammar, it follows that all human languages have this type of system. (p. 4)

As defined in the quote above, in linguistics — and for purposes here — the word *grammar* means the phonetic, phonological, morphological, syntactic and semantic systems of a language. Therefore, if English is defined and classified as a Germanic language based on a criterion of continuity in the rules of grammar, then it stands to reason that "Black English" is defined and classified as a dialect of English because there is continuity in the grammar of "Black English" and the English of non-Blacks.

There is, however, an incongruence in the empirical evidence. Those who believe that Black America's language is a dialect of "English" have not documented the existence of a single Black dialect in the African diaspora that has been formed on an English grammar base (Jahn, 1961).

For the sake of argument, let us accept the view of some that "Black English" is a hybrid dialect invented by English-speaking European people during the colonial era as a "contact vernacular" or trade "lingua franca." If one accepts this view, the dialect would have to be based on the grammar of the "English" language. English-speaking people would not have known the grammar of the Niger-Congo African languages and thus could not have invented a hybrid dialect on an African grammar base.

The problem with this view is that there is not a single example of a hybrid dialect that uses African words superimposed on an English grammar. If this view were valid, surely there would be at least one such dialect documented in the diaspora of Niger-Congo African slaves taken by the English.

The fact is, when one analyzes the grammars of the so-called "Black English" dialect and the English spoken by the Europeans and Euro-Americans, the grammars are not the same. While there has been extensive borrowing or adoption of English and other European words, the grammar of the language of the descendants of Niger-Congo African slaves follows the grammar rules of the Niger-Congo African languages (see Jahn, 1961, p. 194; Alleyne, 1971). In other words, based on a criterion of continuity in the rules of grammar, there is no empirical evidence that "Black English" ever existed.

An alternative thesis could be that it is not continuity in the rules of "grammar" but the etymology and continuity of the "lexicon" that is the criterion for defining and classifying languages as being related. Logically, if the etymology of the lexicon is the criterion for establishing familial kinship, and the bulk of the vocabulary of "Black English" has been borrowed or adopted from the English language stock, then "Black English" is a dialect of English (see Romaine, 1994, pp. 163–165).

But if one uses such a criterion one must ask: Why is there a double standard? It is universally accepted that English has borrowed the bulk of its lexicon from the Romance or Latin language family. Yet English is not classified as being a Latin or Romance language but as a Germanic language.

Actually, the use of *vocabulary* to classify the language of African Americans is just as incongruent. That is, since Latin and French are the origin of the bulk of the English lexicon, how is it that African-American speech is even classified as an English dialect at all? If the dominant lexifier of the English language is Latin and French, then ipso facto the etymology of the dominant lexicon of so-called "Black English" is Latin and French. By this criterion, it logically follows that the dialect being called

"Black English" would more properly be called "Black Latin" or "Black French."

There is however, another possible definition or meaning of the phrase "Black English" — one that does not hinge on the criteria for classifying a language but rather one that has to do with how the word *Black* is perceived and defined. Those who posit this view contend that "any definition of Black English is closely bound to the problem of defining 'Blackness.'" They posit that there is a wide range of characteristics and experiences among Black people, from those in the street culture to those in the middle class.

Concomitantly, there are many Blacks who are exposed to the English of the upper class and of educated native English speakers, while other Blacks have only been exposed to the dialects of English of the poorer whites. And there are Black people who, though they have not lived in close proximity to Euro-Americans, have had the benefit of an excellent English language instruction.

The argument is made that "Black English" is not merely the Black idiom of the particular English dialect to which a Black has been exposed. "Black English" refers to the English spoken by a Black person who has "mastered" and is ideally competent in his or her use of the grammar and vocabulary of Standard American English.

It must be stressed, however, that this "Black English" is not the "Black English" that is often described as having characteristics distinctively different from the Standard American English idiom. In fact, in terms of its grammatical structure, the "Black English" spoken and written by Blacks who are fluent or ideally competent in Standard American English is identical to that of the Euro-American's Standard American English.

Thus, a critical examination of the literature reveals there are at least three distinct connotations that the appellation "Black English" can have. The first is that "Black English" is a dialect of African Americans that is "based" on mutant ("baby talk") Old English and Middle English archaic forms. The second connotation is that "Black English" is a hybrid dialect of African Americans that has as its genesis the transactional or pidgin/

creole language of the West and Niger-Congo African slaves (see Joiner, 1979). The third connotation is that "Black English" is the English spoken by mulattoes, house Negroes, and Black bilinguals who have "mastered" the grammar and vocabulary of Standard English.

Let us now turn to the perspective of the Africologist or Africanist scholars that the native language or mother tongue of the descendants of West and Niger-Congo African slaves is not a dialect of English.

THE MEANING AND MISUSE
OF THE APPELLATION EBONICS

The term *Ebonics* was coined in January 1973 by Dr. Robert L. Williams, a Professor of Psychology at Washington University in St. Louis, Missouri. Dr. Williams coined the term *Ebonics* during a small group discussion with several African American psychologists, linguists, and speech communications professionals attending a conference convened by Dr. Williams entitled "Cognitive and Language Development of the Black Child."

Etymologically, "Ebonics" is a compound of two words: "Ebony," which means "Black," and "phonics," which means "sounds." Thus Ebonics means, literally, "Black Sounds." As an all encompassing, nonpejorative label, the term *Ebonics* refers to the language of West African, Caribbean, and U.S. slave descendants of Niger-Congo African origin (see Williams 1975, p. 100).

In the sense that Ebonics includes both the verbal and paralinguistic communications of African-American people, this means that Ebonics represents an underlying psychological thought process. Hence, the nonverbal sounds, cues, gestures, and so on that are systematically used in the process of communication by African-American people are encompassed by the term as well. This is the original and only intended meaning of the term *Ebonics*.

The consensus among the African-American scholars at the conference was that, owing to their history as slave descendants of West and Niger-Congo African origin, and to the extent that African Americans have been born into, reared in, and continue to live in linguistic environments that are different from the Euro-American English-speaking population, African-American children are not from home environments in which the English language is dominant. The consensus was that, as evidenced by phonetic, phonological, morphological, and syntactical patterns, African-American speech does not follow the grammar rules of English. Rather, it is a West and Niger-Congo African deep structure that has been retained. It is this African deep structure that causes African-American children to score poorly on standardized scales of English proficiency.

In essence, the "genesis" or "origin" of the African-American child's language is the West and Niger-Congo languages of Africa. While being segregated, denied, deprived, and socioeconomically disadvantaged certainly has limited the African American's exposure to and acquisition of Standard English, segregation and poverty is not the "origin" or root cause of the African-American child's limited English proficiency.

When the term *Ebonics* was coined it was not as a mere synonym for the more commonly used appellation *Black English*. Rather, the term *Ebonics* was a repudiation of the lie that Niger-Congo Africans had no fully developed languages originally and that the genesis of human speech for English-speaking African slaves is an Old English "baby talk" or European-invented pidgin/creole vernacular.

AN AFRICAN GRAMMAR WITH ENGLISH WORDS

Since the 1930s, a number of scholars have posited that African-American speech is an African Language System. These include Carter G. Woodson, (1933), Lorenzo Turner (1973), Melville Herskovits (1941, 1958), Janheinz Jahn (1961), Nathan Hare (1965), L. Merriwhether and Adrian Dove (1967), Mervyn Alleyne (1971), Robert Twiggs (1973), Ernie Smith (1974), Robert L. Williams (1975), Anita DeFrantz (1975), Garrett X. Duncan (1995), Aisha Blackshire-Belay (1996), and Karen Crozier (1996). These scholars have consistently maintained that in the hybridization process, it was the grammar of the Niger-Congo African languages that was dominant and that the extensive word borrowing from the English stock does not make Ebonics a dialect of English. In fact, they argue, because it is an African Language System, it is improper to apply terminology that has been devised to describe the grammar of English to describe African-American linguistic structures.

For example, the scholars who view African-American speech as a dialect of English describe the absent final consonant clusters as being "lost," "reduced," "weakened," "simplified," "deleted," or "omitted" consonant phoneme.

But viewed as an African Language System that has adopted European words, African-American speech is described by Africologists as having retained the canonical form, or shape, of the syllable structure of the Niger-Congo African languages. Thus, in Ebonics homogeneous consonant clusters tend not to occur. This is not because the final phoneme has been "lost," "reduced," "weakened," "simplified," "deleted" or "omitted," but because *they never existed in the first place.* Hence it is by relexification (that is, "the replacement of a vocabulary item in a language with a word from another, without a change in the grammar," — see Dillard, 1972) that in Ebonics English words such as *west, best, test, last* and *fast* become *wes, bes, tes, las* and *fas*; the words *land, band, sand* and *hand* become *lan, ban, san* and *han*; the words *left, lift, drift* and *swift* become *lef, lif, drif* and *swif*— and so forth.

Similarly, the canonical form, or shape, of syllable structure of Ebonics is that of the Niger-Congo languages of Africa, that is, a strongly consonant vowel, consonant vowel (CV, CV) vocalic pattern. Again, by relexification, in Ebonics entire sentences will have a CV, CV vocalic pattern. In Ebonics a sentence such as, "Did you eat yet?" will exhibit the CV vocalic pattern /ǰ i ǰ E t/ or /ǰ u w i ǰ E t/. The reply "No" or "Naw did you?" will exhibit the CV vocalic pattern /n ò ǰ u/. The sentence "Did you eat your jello?" will by relexification exhibit the CV pattern /ǰ u w i č o ǰ E l o/.

Because they view African-American speech as an English dialect, Eurocentric scholars contend that in sentences such as "You the teacher" and "That teacher she mean" a copula verbal or the verb *to be* has been "deleted," "dropped," or "omitted." In contrast, because Africologists view the language of African descendants as an African Language System, they contend that there has been no "deleted," "dropped," or "omitted" copula or verb *to be* in the sentences "You the teacher" and "That teacher she mean." As an African Language System that has an equational or equative clause phrase structure, the verb *to be never existed in the first place.*

Absolutely convinced that it is a vernacular dialect of English, Eurocentric scholars have also posited the existence of "double subjects" in so-called Black English. Viewing Ebonics as an English dialect, Eurocentric scholars mistakenly divide sentences such as "That teacher she mean" and "My sister she smart" into noun phrase (NP) and verb phrase (VP) constituents — as English would be properly divided. In contrast, equally convinced that Black American Language is in fact an African linguistic system, the Africologists do not divide sentences such as "That teacher she mean" and "My sister she smart" into NP and VP constituents. As an African system, the division of an equative clause sentence structure is into "topic" and "comment" constituents. Hence, the pronoun *she* that follows the common nouns *teacher* and *sister* in each sentence is not a constituent of the "topic" segment of the sentence. It is a recapitulative pronoun that belongs to the "comment" segment.

In sum, Ebonics is not a dialect of English. The term *Ebonics* and other Afrocentric appellations such as *Pan African Language* and *African Language Systems* all refer to the linguistic continuity of Africa in Black America. Eurocentric scholars use the term *Ebonics* as a synonym for "Black English." In doing so, they reveal an ignorance of the origin and meaning of the term *Ebonics* that is so profound that their confusion is pathetic. (See especially the articles appearing in the Weddington edited issue of the *Journal of Black Studies* June 1979.)

Eurocentric scholars lack any logical explanation for why, in the entire African diaspora, there is not a single hybrid English and Niger-Congo African dialect that has an English grammar as its base with African words superimposed. They also lack any logical reasons for using vocabulary as their basis for classifying Black American speech, while using grammar as their basis for classifying English. In the process, they are exposed for the academic charlatans they are.

The imperative, however, is to recognize that all pupils are equal and hence, all pupils should to be treated equally. Limited-English-Proficient (LEP) Asian-American, Hispanic-American, Native-American, and other pupils who come from backgrounds where a language other than English is dominant are provided bilingual education and English as a second language (ESL) programs to address their LEP needs. African-American LEP pupils should not, because of their race, be subtly dehumanized, stigmatized, discriminated against or denied. LEP African-American pupils are equally entitled to be provided bilingual education and ESL programs to address their LEP needs.

John Rickford, a linguistics professor at Stanford University since 1980, was born in Georgetown, Guyana, and received his doctorate in linguistics from the University of Pennsylvania.

For the past twenty-five years, he has focused on the relation between language and culture, developing models that use sociology, anthropology, and linguistics to explain and resolve educational problems. He is currently co-authoring a book on Ebonics, African-American Vernacular English, and co-editing three other books.

Rickford was interviewed by Clarence Johnson of the *San Francisco Chronicle*. The interview originally appeared February 26, 1997. © 1997 *San Francisco Chronicle*, reprinted with permission.

There has been furious debate over whether Ebonics is really a language. Where do you stand on that? What criteria qualifies dialect as language?

The decision about whether two varieties are languages or different dialects is usually made more on social and political grounds rather than on linguistic grounds. One example of that is the fact that different Chinese varieties that are mutually incomprehensible, such as Mandarin and Cantonese, are regarded as different dialects of the same language, whereas various Scandinavian varieties, such as Norwegian and Swedish, which actually share a lot of vocabulary, are regarded as different languages.

But this is not an airtight measure, and a lot of subjective factors fall into place. There used to be a method where you would look at how many words are shared between two languages. If it was 80 percent or more, you'd say they were dialects of the same language rather than different languages.

By those criteria, I would probably say that African American vernac-

59

ular English or Ebonics is most accurately described as a dialect rather than a totally separate language. But having said that, I would have to say it is the most distinctive dialect in the United States and the one that has gotten the attention of linguistics more than any other for the last thirty years. It's really quite different from other dialects in a number of respects.

In what ways?

Particularly in the grammar, in the verb phrase, in the ways of expressing time. The feature a lot of people talk about is the use of the invariant *be* for habitual aspects, as in "I be walking" or "I be dancing."

I need to stress the restriction to the habitual aspect, because people make fun of the language by using *be* to refer to an incident that is only happening now — as if I were to say "Clarence Johnson be sitting in the chair across from me right now." But as a matter of fact, speakers don't use it like that. They would say something like "Every Sunday morning, Clarence Johnson always be sitting here," referring to the habitual.

Then there is the stress *been*, which refers to a state or action that has been in place a long time ago. Somebody might ask: "Did you pay off that bill for that stereo?" and you reply "Oh, I been paid for that."

I did a study on *been*, and most whites didn't understand it. If you offer a sentence like "Is she married?" and the other person says "Aw, she been married," the question is: Is she married now or not? Most whites would (think), "No, she's not married," while most Blacks would (think), "Yes, she's married, in fact she is very married and has been for a long time." So you see, this could cause some confusion.

Can you speak to the historical origins of Black dialect?

There is a strong debate about the origins of African-American vernacular. One position argues that when African Americans came to this country, they essentially acquired the dialect of whites who were here at the time. The other position is that when slaves first came over here, the acquisition of English was not as straightforward.

In fact, slaves were often separated from models of English usage, and in the course of acquiring English, developed first a pidgin and then a creole language — a mixed, simplified variety of English strongly influenced by their own native languages.

Now, you can view the result as a language problem, or you can view it as language creativity, because it is a creative response to a language-learning situation.

What is significant, unique, or different about the development of language in African Americans?

It has always struck me as interesting that while masters were busy trying to separate slaves from different linguistic backgrounds so they could not communicate with each other, throughout the New World slaves were busy creating (languages) that allowed them to communicate with each other. Slaves would develop ways of talking with each other. It is much like the use of spirituals by people who were running away. The song "Wade in the Water" meant that the master was sending bloodhounds or something after you so, to be safe, stay in the river.

I'd be surprised if it weren't true that Africans used this language to talk among themselves. Whether they only developed it for that purpose is harder to say. But clearly once it was in place, they used it to pass messages among themselves.

Has there been a social or economic impact on African Americans for speaking something other than so-called Standard English?

It's hard to gauge. But if you talk about the world of work or in the world of school, a speaker who is more restricted to Ebonics is perhaps restricted in the range of jobs and range of success that he or she might achieve. But other people are fond of pointing out that there are those who speak more Standard English, and they still don't do so well. You don't want to chalk up all the limitations that African Americans face to language. Still, if a person cannot really show mastery of the Standard English, he or she is likely to be more limited in terms of employment and education.

But a lot of the fuss over Ebonics over the past month has really resulted from a misunderstanding of what the Oakland school board was trying to do. The function of (the Oakland) program is to help kids to master Standard English by taking into account the vernacular they come to school with.

Language is often seen as a way to gauge intelligence. How accurate is it as such?

It's definitely not an accurate gauge of intelligence. It may well be a reflection of the amount of education one has. But you should be very careful about assuming that equals intelligence, because speakers can display all kinds of intelligence in all kinds of varieties of language. So you have to be careful not to confuse the two.

The problem with all this Ebonics stuff over the years is that people have preconceptions and misconceptions and have made mistakes. A teacher might assume that somebody who speaks Ebonics is dumb, but a person can be a lot sharper than they appear. In fact, we have a lot of clear evidence that attitudes shape expectations and a teacher's expectations shape performance. It's a very dangerous kind of mistake to make.

With that in mind, why is the Ebonics debate important? Does it have ramifications beyond Black children or the African-American community?

I'm sure it does, but I want to comment on the ramifications within the Black community because they are so huge. The fact of the matter is, whether we look at Oakland or any inner city, African-American kids are really doing disastrously in education. That is the problem people should have been focusing on. This certainly is where Oakland started.

They started with the fact that African-American kids in the district were doing worse than everybody else. And if you look around the country, you will find very dramatic evidence that every year inner-city African-American kids stay in school, the worse they do relative to mainstream populations. This was pointed out years ago, and you can see it particularly in reading and language arts.

In testimony before a congressional subcommittee, data showed that at nine years old, African-American kids are 27 points behind in reading. By the time you get to seventeen years old, they are 37 points behind. So the more schooling they get, the worse they do.

The reason is because, by and large, the education African Americans are getting is below par. And that's been the case for African-American kids for at least the past three decades. And if you look at the kids who are doing worse in the system, they are very fluent speakers of Ebonics.

I'd be the first to agree with those who say this problem is not just about Ebonics. It's about inadequate facilities and lack of supplies. It's about pay for teachers, particularly for those who work in districts with larger numbers of Black speakers, who are not paid as much as teachers in other districts. These are vital problems that need to be fixed.

But there's also a language component to the problem. And if you were to control all those other factors and you didn't take the language factors into account, you would not have much success. And that is a big issue that until now, nobody has faced up to.

So the Oakland school board was not wrong to make such an issue of what many people see merely as schoolchildren's poor grammar?

The Oakland task force on Ebonics didn't set out to give linguists a field day. It was important for them to look at this issue. Teaching approaches that take into account the vernacular dialect of kids work more effectively than those that don't.

It's almost paradoxical. One might think that if you ignored the vernacular and concentrated on Standard English, you'd have more success. But in fact, it's the other way around. There are a lot of studies that show this — and they are not new. Four of them were actually done in Sweden in the late 1950s.

As an African American, I have many friends who are highly educated professionals who speak Standard English on their daily jobs. But when we come together off the job, we ease into a Black dialogue that we otherwise would never speak. Why do we do that?

It's like having a hammer for one kind of function and a saw for another. You might say, "Well I'll just use a tool." But some tools work better for some purposes than others. No person just operates in the world of work and school. You have to go back home to your people, to your mom or brother and sister.

And people who grow away from their vernacular often find their lives uncomfortable. For example, a person goes away to England and comes back speaking the King's English, people will give him a hard time. Behind his back, people will say "Who does he think he is?"

So if Ebonics was not functional — marking out a Black identity, creating bonds of solidarity and friendship, allowing people to relax and let themselves go — it wouldn't survive. It would not be around today if it did not fulfill those and some other functions. The different (language) varieties we have exist because they are not equally good for all the different functions.

So who speaks Ebonics?

What's beautiful about the example you just gave is the fact that there is nobody who speaks its features 100 percent of the time. If you look at the most different variety of Ebonics, it's probably spoken more by the working and lower classes. But the thing is, almost all African Americans speak some variety of it to a greater or lesser extent. Even Rev. Jesse Jackson when making some of his speeches will have a number of rhetorical features of African-American English-speaking styles. He'll use some of the vocabulary or intonations. That's why when you turn on the radio, if you didn't know that it was Jesse Jackson, you nonetheless would know that it was a Black speaker.

Senator Lauch Faircloth, R-N. C., recently called Ebonics "absurd . . . political correctness run out of control." Why is much of America having such a tough time accepting the notion that Black Americans have a language unto themselves?

Some of it has to do with nonstandard dialects in general. All over the world, they tend to be disparaged. Sometimes people even associate it with personal values like laziness, or even moral degeneracy. As though if speakers just made a greater effort, they could switch from their dialects to standard languages.

In the case of Ebonics, a couple of things come into play. It originated in the days of slavery. So there is an association with the past of African Americans that is very troubling to some people. In addition, there's this constant tension between the urge to be assimilated and yet to be different. W. E. B. Du Bois talked about it years ago in terms of a push-pull, love-hate relationship to white America.

A white colleague has a book coming out that includes a chapter called "The Real Trouble with Black English." And the real trouble, as she puts it, is that the existence of Black English itself gives testimony to the fact that African Americans have not completely assimilated. They haven't melted into the melting pot, partly because of social and economic factors and partly because of a will to maintain a distinctive identity. So to the extent ongoing segregation shows up in different patterns of language, it's an embarrassment. And people don't like to have these differences pointed out.

It seems everybody is united — even the Oakland school board — in ridding Black students of Black Language patterns. What's wrong with African Americans having a language or dialect of their own?

Novelist Toni Morrison, in writing for *The New Republic*, once said that one of the worst possible things for (Blacks) to do would be to lose that language. It's a terrible thing when a child comes to school with five present tenses, only to meet a language that is less than him. And then he is told terrible things about his language — which is him. She was trying to show that there is this whole rich way of expressing certain things in terms of time, and tense and aspect, which most people are not aware of.

We educators have learned that it's not possible to legislate the use of language, certainly not in the community or at home. It has a life of its own. People say, "Well, you are going to try to wipe out this vernacular." But that doesn't make any sense, because we can't. We know from experience.

So you ask, why does the vernacular persist? It is because it feeds into a whole alternative set of identities and purposes that speakers find rewarding and valuable.

The language, only the language. . . . It's the thing black people love so much — the saying of words, holding them on the tongue, experimenting with them, playing with them. It's a love, a passion. Its function is like a preacher's: to make you stand up out of your seat, make you lose yourself and hear yourself. The worst of all possible things that could happen would be to lose that language. There are certain things I cannot say without recourse to my language.

Toni Morrison
The New Republic *magazine, 1981*

If Black English Isn't a Language, Then Tell Me, What Is?

JAMES BALDWIN

The argument concerning the use, or the status, or the reality, of Black English is rooted in American history and has absolutely nothing to do with the question the argument supposes itself to be posing. The argument has nothing to do with language itself but with the role of language. Language, incontestably, reveals the speaker. Language, also, far more dubiously, is meant to define the other — and, in this case, the other is refusing to be defined by a language that has never been able to recognize him.

People evolve a language in order to describe and thus control their circumstances or in order not to be submerged by a reality that they cannot articulate. (And, if they cannot articulate it, they are submerged.) A Frenchman living in Paris speaks a subtly and crucially different language from that of the man living in Marseilles; neither sounds very much like a man living in Quebec; and they would all have great difficulty in apprehending what the man from Guadeloupe, or Martinique, is saying, to say nothing of the man from Senegal — although the "common" language of all these areas is French. But each has paid, and is paying, a different price for this "common" language, in which, as it turns out, they are not saying and cannot be saying, the same things: They each have very different realities to articulate or control.

What joins all languages, and all men, is the necessity to confront life, in order, not inconceivably, to outwit death: The price for this is the acceptance, and achievement, of one's temporal identity. So that, for example, though it is not taught in the schools (and this has the potential of becoming a political issue) the south of France still clings to its ancient and musical Provençal, which resists being described as a "dialect." And much of the tension in the Basque countries, and in Wales, is due to the Basque and Welsh determination not to allow their languages to be destroyed. This determination also feeds the flames in Ireland, for among the many indignities the Irish have been forced to undergo at English hands is the English contempt for their language.

LANGUAGE AND POWER

It goes without saying, then, that language is also a political instrument, means, and proof of power. It is the most vivid and crucial key to identity: It reveals the private identity, and connects one with, or divorces one from, the larger public, or communal identity. There have been, and are, times, and places, when to speak a certain language could be dangerous, even fatal. Or, one may speak the same language, but in such a way that one's antecedents are revealed, or (one hopes) hidden. This is true in France, and is absolutely true in England: The range (and reign) of accents on that damp little island make England coherent for the English and totally incomprehensible for everyone else. To open your mouth in England is (if I may use Black English) to "put your business in the street": You have confessed your parents, your youth, your school, your salary, your self-esteem and, alas, your future.

Now, I do not know what white Americans would sound like if there had never been any Black people in the United States, but they would not sound the way they sound. *Jazz*, for example, is a very specific sexual term, as in *jazz me baby*, but white people purified it into the Jazz Age. *Sock it to me*, which means, roughly, the same thing, has been adopted by Nathaniel Hawthorne's descendants with no qualms or hesitations at all, along with *let it all hang out* and *right on*! *Beat to his socks*, which was once the Black's most total and despairing image of poverty, was transformed into a thing called the Beat Generation which phenomenon was, largely, composed of *uptight*, middle-class white people, imitating poverty, trying to *get down*, to *get with it*, doing their *thing*, doing their despairing best to be *funky*, which we, the Blacks never dreamed of doing — *we were* funky, baby, like *funk* was going out of style.

Now, no one can eat his cake, and have it, too, and it is late in the day to attempt to penalize Black people for having created a language that permits the nation its only glimpse of reality, a language without which the nation would be even more *whipped* than it is.

A CREATION OF THE BLACK DIASPORA

I say that this present skirmish is rooted in American history and it is. Black English is the creation of the Black diaspora. Blacks came to the United States chained to each other, but from different tribes: Neither could speak the other's language. If two Black people at that bitter hour of the world's history, had been able to speak to each other, the institution of chattel slavery could never have lasted as long as it did. Subsequently, the slave was given, under the eye, and the gun, of his master, Congo Square, and the Bible — or, in other words, and under these conditions, the slave began the formation of the Black church, and it is within this unprecedented tabernacle that Black English began to be formed. This was not, merely, as in the European example, the adoption of a foreign tongue, but an alchemy that transformed ancient elements into new language: *A language comes into existence by means of brutal necessity, and the rules of the language are dictated by what the language must convey.*

There was a moment, in time, and in this place, when my brother, or my mother, or my father, or my sister, had to convey to me, for example, the danger in which I was standing from the white man standing just behind me, and to convey this with a speed, and in a language, that the white man could not possibly understand, and that, indeed, he cannot understand, until today. He cannot afford to understand it. This understanding would reveal to him too much about himself, and smash that mirror before which he has been frozen for so long.

Now, if this passion, this skill, this (to quote Toni Morrison) "sheer intelligence," this incredible music, the mighty achievement of having brought a people utterly unknown to, or despised by "history" — to have brought this people to their present, troubled, troubling, and unassailable and unanswerable place — if this absolutely unprecedented journey does not indicate that Black English is a language, I am curious to know what definition of language is to be trusted.

A people at the center of the Western world, and in the midst of so hostile a population, has not endured and transcended by means of what is patronizingly called a "dialect." We, the Blacks, are in trouble, certainly, but we are not doomed, and we are not inarticulate because we are not compelled to defend a morality that we know to be a lie.

The brutal truth is that the bulk of the white people in America never had any interest in educating Black people, except as this could serve white purposes. It is not the Black child's language that is in question, it is not his language that is despised: It is his experience. A child cannot be taught by anyone who despises him, and a child cannot afford to be fooled. A child cannot be taught by anyone whose demand, essentially, is that the child repudiate his experience, and all that gives him sustenance, and enter a limbo in which he will no longer be Black, and in which he knows that he can never become white. Black people have lost too many Black children that way.

And, after all, finally, in a country with standards so untrustworthy, a country that makes heroes of so many criminal mediocrities, a country unable to face why so many of the nonwhite are in prison, or on the needle, or standing, futureless, in the streets — it may very well be that both the child, and his elder, have concluded that they have nothing whatever to learn from the people of a country that has managed to learn so little.

Ebonics: Myths and Realities

MARY RHODES HOOVER

African-American communities are in educational crisis. Given the well-documented history of schools' failure to teach African-American children, the Oakland school board's resolution on Ebonics is a rare position in American education.

The board decided that Ebonics/African-American Language should be used as a bridge to teaching Standard English. The goal is realizable, yet several myths abound: that Ebonics is limited as a tool to teaching Standard English because it is just "bad grammar," "lazy pronunciation," and slang; that there is no research linking Ebonics to education; that literacy problems among African-American children are really the parents' fault; and that the debate over Ebonics has been useless.

MYTH #1: EBONICS IS JUST BAD GRAMMAR, LAZY PRONUNCIATION, AND SLANG.

The term *Ebonics* was coined by Dr. Robert Williams at a conference in 1973 (see Ernie Smith, page 49). The language itself has existed since the arrival of Blacks in the United States, according to Dr. Lorenzo Turner, whose seminal work *Africanisms in the Gullah Dialect* lists 4,000 African words in the Gullah language on islands off the coast of South Carolina.

Many who condemn Ebonics refer to it as "bad grammar," "lazy pronunciation," or slang. However, linguist Dell Hymes notes that, viewed sociolinguistically, language is much more than characteristics such as grammar or pronunciation (phonology). In fact, Ebonics/African American Language has a number of other characteristics, including semantics, intonation, favored genres, sociolinguistic rules, speaking style, learning and teaching style, and world view/themes. It is important that teachers be given a broad description of the language of Ebonics in order to understand its complexity, the complexity of its speakers, and the role of Ebonics in teaching language arts. Following are examples of some of the characteristics of Ebonics. (For more detailed information on the structure of Ebonics, see Asante, 1990; Baugh, 1983; Smitherman, 1977, 1986; Turner, 1969; Smith, 1974; Rose, 1994; Hoover, Dabney, & Lewis, 1990.)

Grammar and Pronunciation. An example of Ebonics grammar is the habitual use of the verb, as in "I be going to church," which means "I go habitually." West African verbs have similar structures. A phonological example is the fact that consonants and consonant clusters are often not a part of the Ebonics syllable, for example, "I 'on know" for "I don't know," or "aight" for "all right."

Semantics. A vocabulary/semantics example is the use of inversion, as when a beautiful dress is described as "stupid" or something good is called "bad."

Intonation. The African-American speaker has a wide range in his/her tone, much wider than for whites — for example, Dr. Martin Luther King's "I have a dreeeeam today." It is this Africanized intonation that informs us that a person we can hear but not see is African American.

Favored Genres. Favored genres for Ebonics speakers are drama, proverbs, and poetry/rap.

Sociolinguistic Rules. Such rules include the avoidance of taboo words — layovers from Southern apartheid — such as "boy," "you people." Another such rule is the approval of using Ebonics in oral or casual situations but not in written or formal situations, such as in textbooks.

Speaking Style and Learning and Teaching Style. Examples of speaking style are dramatic repetition ("I Have a Dream"), the Call and Response Style, and the use of rhyming and circular narratives. Under learning and teaching style, we find the use of Audience Participation and Structure, such as the use of structured phonics reading methodology, which is a reading method frequently and effectively used in teaching the bilingual/bidialectical Ebonics speaker.

Worldview/Themes. As defined by Brazilian educator Paulo Freire, generative themes are those themes that stir a culture to learn faster. For Ebonics speakers, such themes include affirmation (such as self-determination), protest, the wretchedness of oppression, and the avoidance of stereotypes, according to Sterling Brown, late professor of literature at Howard University. For example, there are four prevalent stereotypes of African Americans: the Exotic Primitive, the Contented Slave, the Brute, and the Comic. Several issues in the Ebonics debate can only be explained by the need to avoid these stereotypes. For example, the rejection of the Oakland school board Ebonics resolution by some African Americans is probably due to the desire to avoid the stereotypes of the Exotic Primitive and the Comic, with the Exotic Primitive perceived as so different and exotic that his/her language is a joke.

MYTH #2: THERE IS NO RESEARCH LINKING EBONICS TO EDUCATION.

Research supports the Standard English Proficiency program (SEP) used by the Oakland district. The program stresses Ebonics as a bridge to teaching literacy to African-American students. Its emphasis is on teaching students Standard English speaking skills, on teaching the teachers about the Ebonics speakers' language and culture, and on teaching reading through "Superliteracy," which endorses phonics in addition to eight other components (Bazely, 1996). If there is a main culprit in the reading problems facing Ebonics speakers, it is the flight from phonics.

There is a thirty-year track record for teaching reading to Ebonics speakers, from Jean Chall's *Learning to Read: The Great Debate* in 1967, to *Successful Black and Minority Schools,* a 1990 book edited by myself and Norma Dabney and Shirley Lewis, to B. R. Foorman's work at the University of Houston in 1995. The record is clear: African-American students who speak Ebonics can be taught to read at high levels using any one of several phonics-based reading programs. These highly structured, intensive approaches are appropriate for Ebonics-speaking students because they are similar to foreign language teaching methods — with students first being exposed to regular patterns (phonics), then passages written in these patterns.

The only battery of tests for Ebonics speakers, formally published in the 1996 *Handbook of Tests and Measurements for Black Populations*, was conducted by Stanford University's Program on Teaching and Linguistic Pluralism from 1969 to 1980. The research involved more than one hundred teachers and hundreds of students in California, New York, Ohio, and Florida. It found that teachers who had highly positive attitudes and expectations toward Ebonics speakers, as well as more information about Ebonics characteristics and how to teach such speakers, were those whose students gained the most over a five-month test period. A second Stanford study, also cited in the 1996 *Handbook*, showed that the ability to discriminate between Standard English and Ebonics significantly correlates with reading ability among African-American students.

Publishers, however, have a history of marketing materials based on flimsy research for the sole purpose of making money. This can be seen in the recent "whole language" debacle, in which a method devoid of any research regarding its effectiveness was foisted on public schools. Though all students suffered from this educational malpractice, African-American and other students with different languages in their backgrounds were particular victims. In 1994, California became the first state to legislate that teachers must have a "balanced" approach to the teaching of reading, one that includes both literature and phonics.

MYTH #3: LITERACY PROBLEMS AMONG AFRICAN-AMERICAN CHILDREN ARE REALLY THE PARENTS' FAULT.

Successful schools do not rely on parents to teach their children to read (Hoover, Dabney & Lewis, 1990). In actuality, it is the responsibility of the school administration to be the catalyst for changing the schools and ensuring appropriate teaching of literacy to African-American children.

Parents and community members, however, can force substantive change. Although curriculum theory textbooks used by schools of education never mention the role of community boards and organizations in curriculum reform, the Oakland Board of Education has shown that communities can force curriculum reform.

African-American parents and community members have fought for literacy throughout history — most notably during the days of slavery, when it was illegal in slave states to teach African Americans to read, and on through the Freedom Schools during the civil rights and Black Power era, the formation of independent Black schools in the 1960s and 1970s, and reforms in some public schools in more recent decades. Yet these movements have often been unimplemented, misimplemented, or ignored by public schools administrations — to the extent that there is no school district in the country performing at level in which the students are predominantly African American or other students of color.

MYTH #4: THE DEBATE OVER EBONICS HAS BEEN USELESS.

Yes, the children suffer while we debate. Structural linguists, sociolinguists, and applied linguists battle over terminology. Some linguists criticize everyone. Still others are busy writing "dialect readers." And many educators dismiss the entire issue as irrelevant and take very little interest in solving the problems of Black illiteracy.

The Ebonics project, with its emphasis on phonic-inclusive literacy methods and on improving teacher attitudes (one of the major characteristics of a successful school), may solve the problem of Black illiteracy — if the recommendations of the Task Force for African-American Education are implemented. For administrators, teachers, parents, and community activists who decide to implement the research on bringing African-American students up to and above grade level, the research — available through the education database ERIC and in library card catalogs — has been there since 1967.

If public schools are to survive, they must find a solution to the systematic failure to teach African-American children. Parents consider reading to be the most important outcome of schooling, and employers view it as one of the most important skills for a worker in the twenty-first century. Yet discussions of the appropriate methods for teaching literacy to African-American children continue to be an invisible topic in school districts.

3   Classroom Implications

School itself tended to be lots better than those bus rides.
Chemistry was good; I still liked that. And math. English, too,
especially oratory and poetry. . . . So I memorized poems for
the oratory contests. Paul Laurence Dunbar's dialect poetry
and Langston Hughes, the great black poet from Joplin,
Missouri, and Harlem, New York. I won first prize reciting
Rudyard Kipling's "If."

Joycelyn Elders
from Joycelyn Elders, M.D.: From Sharecropper's Daughter
to Surgeon General of the United States of America

Embracing Ebonics and Teaching Standard English
An Interview with Oakland Teacher Carrie Secret

This article is adapted from an interview with Carrie Secret, a fifth-grade teacher at Prescott Elementary School in the Oakland Unified School District. Prescott had been the only school in the system where a majority of teachers had voluntarily agreed to adopt the Standard English Proficiency program, a statewide initiative that acknowledges the systematic, rule-governed nature of "Black English" while helping children to learn Standard English. Secret was interviewed by Barbara Miner, managing editor of *Rethinking Schools*.

How long have you been a teacher and how long have you been at Prescott Elementary School?

After I left Omaha in February 1966, I was hired in Oakland and assigned to Prescott. Everybody said, "Oh you poor thing, you're assigned to Prescott!" But I've been there thirty-one years because I refused to be transferred. There had been times when excellent teachers left Prescott, but they were never replaced with the same caliber of teacher.

I've never desired to do anything but teach. I have never desired to leave the classroom for any other position. Teaching is my passion. I've taught every grade in elementary school except kindergarten. I now teach fifth grade with a group of children I've had since they were in first grade. I have thirty-one children in my class. One is Lakota Sioux, two are Cambodian, two are Mexican, and twenty-six are African American.

Prescott is one of the Oakland schools that uses the Standard English Proficiency program (SEP). Can you explain the concepts underlying SEP?

The issue gets clouded because the SEP programs vary throughout the state. The most powerful difference is that we in the Oakland SEP, under the inspirational directorship of Nabeehah Shakir, dared to honor and respect Ebonics as the home language that stands on its own rather than as a dialectical form of English. We see and understand that our language patterns and structure come from a family of languages totally unrelated to the Germanic roots of English. In some programs, grammar and drill are strong parts. I think our using second-language learning strategies has more impact on the students. The view is, "We are teaching you a second language, not fixing the home language you bring to school."

There are three cornerstones to our SEP program: culture, language, and literacy. Our program is not just a language program that stresses how well you acquire and speak English. We emphasize the learning of reading by incorporating a strong literacy component. Another crucial issue is that we push students to learn the content language of each area of curriculum. The Oakland SEP program is not just a grammar and drill program but a program that emphasizes language and content and encompasses all areas of curriculum.

Children are not empowered simply because they know subject/verb agreement. That is not powerful for children if they don't have content in which to use the language. Yes, we want the children to speak English and have positive feelings about themselves, but that comes about only when the children know content. It doesn't matter how well you speak if you are not able to participate in and use the language of the content areas during discussion times.

The other issue is culture. If you don't respect the children's culture, you negate their very essence. We in the SEP program draw our cultural components from the work of the Center for Applied Cultural Studies and Educational Achievement (CACSEA) at San Francisco State University. CACSEA is under the directorship of Dr. Wade Nobles, a scholar in African and African-American culture and history, and provides professional development programs for teachers of African-American students. CACSEA's program manager and trainer, Augusta Mann, presents staff development sessions for SEP that focus on the culture of African-American people and uses the culture to enhance reading achievement. The program highlights nine cultural aspects that permeate African-American life: spirituality, resilience, emotional vitality, musicality and rhythm, humanism, communalism, orality and verbal expressiveness, personal style and uniqueness, and realness. These concepts are then presented in conjunction with instructional strategies that have proven to be effective for African-American students.

Are there particular times during the school day when a student is required to speak Standard English?

In fifth grade, I encourage the students to practice English most of the instructional time. I say "encourage" because "required" is a word that sends a message that if you don't use English then you are operating below standard. Let's say that in fifth grade, students are requested and encouraged to speak in English almost all the time.

There's a misconception of the program, created by the media blitz of misinformation. Our mission was and continues to be: embrace and respect Ebonics, the home language of many of our students, and use strategies that will move them to a competency level in English. We never had, nor do we now have, any intention of teaching the home language to students. They come to us speaking the language.

We read literature that has Ebonics language patterns in it. For example, last year in fifth grade we read Joyce Hansen's *Yellow Bird and Me*, and in fourth grade we read her book *The Gift Giver*. The language was Ebonic in structure. The language was the bonding agent for students. The book just felt good to them.

When writing, the students are aware that finished pieces are written in English. The use of Ebonic structures appears in many of their first drafts. When this happens I simply say, "You used Ebonics here. I need you to translate this thought into English." This kind of statement does not negate the child's thought or language.

Before I met Professor Ernie Smith (see essay, page 49), my approach was different. I used the "fix-something-that-was-wrong" approach. I was always calling for the children to say something correct or to fix something to make it right. I now approach the same task from a different perspective that has a more positive effect on my children.

Some days I simply announce: "While you are working I will be listening to how well you use English. In your groups you must call for translation if a member of your group uses an Ebonic Structure." Some days I say, "Girls, you are at Spelman and boys, you are attending More-house College (historically Black colleges). Today you use the language the professors use and expect you to use in your classes, and that language is English."

I once had some visitors come to my class and they said, "We don't hear Ebonics here." But that is because I had explained to my children that company was coming, and when company comes, we practice speaking English. Company is the best time to practice because most of our visitors are from a cultural language context different from ours.

Do you ever allow students to use Ebonics in the classroom?

The word that bothers me is "allow." Students talk. They bring their home language to school. That is their right. If you are concerned about children using Ebonics in the classroom, you will spend the whole day saying, "Translate, translate, translate." So you have to pick times when you are particularly attuned to and calling for English translation.

When the children are working in groups together, say three or four of them, I try to keep them in an English-speaking mode, but I don't prevent them from using Ebonics. I want to give them time enough to talk through their project in their comfortable language. It's like a prewrite to me. But at some point, they have to present their project to me, and these are required to be presented in their best English.

Professor Ernie Smith said something that put things in perspective for me, especially when it comes to how children pronounce words. And that advice is: You do not teach speech at reading time. When children are reading to me, I want to know that they are comprehending what they are reading. So I don't stop them if they don't pronounce words according to the English pronunciation.

But I will listen to the pronunciation and make mental notes. For ex-ample, I might note that Girl X and Boy Y are dropping the final *t*'s off their words — for example saying *lef* for *left* or *bes* for *best*. I then note to myself that I will need to work on that Ebonics feature with the class.

That's another thing. I always do whole group. I don't like programs that single out kids or pull out children. That includes both gifted and talented programs and deficit-model programs.

How do you teach children to understand that they may be dropping consonants when they speak?

I'm lucky in that I have been with these children five years and at a very early age I engaged them in listening to language for the purpose of hearing and understanding the difference between Ebonics and English. However, by the middle of second grade, they were all readers. So at that point it was easy to go to the overhead and show them exactly what they said and then call for the English translation of what they said.

Hearing the language is a crucial step. Children who speak Ebonics do not hear themselves dropping off the "t" for instance. You have to teach them to hear that. So we do a lot of overenunciation when they are small. I also do a lot of dictation where I will dictate a sentence and have the children write what I said, by sound only. I also try to always point out what is Ebonics speech and what is English. Children must first hear and develop an ear for both languages in order to effectively distinguish between the two.

Do you have any tips for teaching reading to Ebonics speakers?

One of my best approaches with young readers is that I read to them a lot. When they were in the early grades, I read when they come in at 8:30, I read after the first recess, I read after lunch, and I read after the second recess. In first grade, I actually read through the reader that they are going to be using. So by the time I give them their readers, in about mid-October, they are not afraid of the book. They know that words are only something that someone else has said and written down.

We also do a lot of home reading in our school: This is part of a schoolwide program called the Just Read program. Every day, the children take home a book and someone is expected to read to them.

I still read to my children in fifth grade. And they are always reading, whether a book, or for a report, or researching information. I also continue to stress reading for pleasure. Basically, I give the children a lot of language and oral listening — and it's attentive listening and inclusive listening where they have to respond back to me so that I know they are listening.

I am strong on phonics, but I embrace, enjoy, and like whole language. But I am also just as strong on phonics. In first grade, I start dictation right away, giving them phonetically pure words to spell back to me or write back to me. And our kindergarten teachers have done a good job preparing the students for us and have explained certain phonics principles, like short vowels and long vowels. They also give the children certain sight words that we want the children to recognize and certain sight words that we want the children to read.

In the early grades, I do a lot of word flash card drills, phrase drills, sentence drills, which may be from the stories I am reading to them. We also have another drill called "read the word, write the word." We sit in a circle and read from a state-developed word list that was developed for each grade. We take a column a day and we read them and write them, and that becomes a standard homework assignment.

I also want the children to move into critical thinking and content. I am one who believes that everything can be taught at one time. So, for example, we have a phonics book that has a lot of pictures for identification and sounds. After the children have completed the page, they have to go back and group at least four pictures together and tell why they grouped them together. Or they might group four pictures that belong together and one that doesn't and explain why. I might also make a connection between the lesson and the children's lives. I will say, "How would you connect the picture to your life, and why?"

How do you use Black literature to help children learn Standard English?

A lot of people emphasize using Black literature and then translating it. I no longer use this strategy because we were always translating Ebonics to English, but rarely, if ever, English to Ebonics. That tended to negate in my mind the equality of the two languages.

I use the literature because of its cultural essence, its beauty. I want the children to be proud that Toni Morrison and Alice Walker are great writers and that Maya Angelou spoke at the president's inauguration. I am not about to take a beautiful piece of Ebonics literature and then translate it into English. You cannot enjoy Langston Hughes if you are worried about translating him. The beauty of our language gets lost in the translation.

It is necessary for our students to become aware that our greatest models for excellent writers wrote fluently in both English and Ebonics. There are beautiful pieces by Langston Hughes and Paul Laurence Dunbar in English as well as in Ebonics. I had students read *An Ante-Bellum Sermon* by Dunbar, which is straight-up Ebonics, and then read *The Seedling*, which is straight-up English. I also use writings by Jeremiah Wright, a minister out of Chicago who delivers magnificent and powerful sermons that contain African and African-American history. He speaks with a rhythm, with an emotional vitality, as he uses high-level vocabulary in his sermons. Hearing him speak, nearly all the children get the message from context. However, they are required to go back and pull out the vocabulary and research each new word. This is a powerful way to get children to use new vocabulary.

These kind of writings tend to fortify children and also give them a lot of language. I believe in giving children a lot of adult, intellectual language rather than "See Spot run" language. I also try to address the culture of all my children. For example, we have read *To Destroy You Is No Loss* by Joan Criddle and *The Clay Marvel* by Minfong Ho, which are about the Cambodian children. We have read *Daniel's Story*, a story about a Jewish child in a concentration camp, and *Remember My Name*, a book about the Native Americans' Trail of Tears experience.

How do you organize your school day?

In the morning, I do a centering opening based on the CACSEA program. Research has shown that if you get children's adrenaline flowing, they get that natural high and then you can teach them anything you want for the next hour and a half. Basically, that ninety minutes is the only time I teach the whole group. The rest of the morning and afternoon, the children are in independent or small-group work study mode.

When they come in the morning, we start by standing behind our chairs and we do some recitations out of our poetry readers. All of these are self-enhancing pieces of poetry, something that touches the children so they get the joy of being in the classroom. After reciting the poetry, we sing songs. We use a variety of music that touches the spirit of the child. For example, we have used *I Believe I Can Fly*, or Whitney Houston's *Step by Step*, and *To Be Loved*, or some Sweet Honey in the Rock. We have used Sounds of Blackness, classical jazz, and even some Bach, Beethoven, and Mozart. We may even do some African dance movement to music by Herbie Hancock or Quincy Jones.

When the energy is high I say, "Now go inside yourself and find your perfect peace and decide what you want to get out of the day and promise yourself that you will get it." Then I tell them to say my name and request what it is they want from me. I think that is very important, because they have the right and the responsibility to keep me straight, just as I try to keep them straight. I am there because an adult has to be with the children, but I try not to have a hierarchy. There needs to be a mutual respect between the teacher and students. My relationship with the students is a high priority with me. We are strongly bonded by love and trust for each other. Our affectionate feelings transcend the classroom and extend out to the families and communities of my students. We outright love and care for each other.

After the centering, the children write in their journals. Sometimes it is on whatever they choose. Sometimes I check to see if they are internalizing a piece we are working on, such as the sermon "What Makes You So Strong?" I ask them to answer that question as it pertains to them, to see if they understand the essence of what makes a person strong. They may write on "What Makes You So Strong Black Child?" or "Cambodian Child" or "Black Teacher." They have to look for the resilience and the strength in themselves and in other people. Can they identify it? Can they pick it out? We write in our journals for about ten minutes. After that I tell them, "Now I am getting ready to teach, and what I teach you have to remember for the rest of your lives." They take notes — they've been taking notes since they were in first grade — in their record-keeping book.

I try to connect my teaching to African proverbs, principles of Kwanzaa and the Virtues of Maat, or a piece of poetry, or a recitation we are working on. A good example is "What Makes You So Strong." The piece refers to 200 million people lost in the Atlantic Ocean during the Middle Passage from Africa to slavery in the West. From that, we talked about the different oceans of the world and the continents they touch, and from there we read books on the Middle Passage, and from there they did an art piece that showed the root of the Middle Passage and the triangular trade from Africa, to America, to England. From there we went into the study of triangles, which led into geometry.

We did more reading on the Middle Passage and slavery, for example, Amos Fortune's *Free Man*. I read excerpts from *Roots* by Alex Haley, where Kunta was in the Middle Passage. From that we went to other history resource books and did a quick come-back report — where different children read different books and come back with what they found. I used the Middle Passage as the basis for the daily oral language lesson, where I write a sentence with a lot of errors that the students have to correct.

We also used the morning recitation as the basis for a math lesson on estimates. I designed a lesson called "Wipe Out." I have them look at different estimates on how many people were lost in the Middle Passage, because in each source (music, sermon, poem, book) there are different numbers ranging from 70 to 200 million. Using a selected estimate, they determine how many countries would be "wiped out" if they lost the same number of people using the present-day population. We worked it with Mexico, United States, and African countries, so that the children could understand exactly what the numbers meant and the impact of the Middle Passage loss.

After the whole-group teaching ends (the students all have the schedule, which is my weekly lesson plan), I tell the children, "I have taught all that I am going to today. Now it is up to you." They know the work they have to do that day, either by themselves or in groups of two, three, or four.

What has been the most encouraging aspect of the Ebonics controversy? The most frustrating?

What is most encouraging is that parents who were ashamed to come to school and talk their language, and parents were actually ashamed — they lost that. They told me, "You know, Miss Secret, until Ebonics came I wouldn't come over here." It was of benefit to the community as well. Even my mother told me, "You know, Carrie, I wish I had only known I had to learn English better, and that it wasn't that I was using bad English."

Then the other thing that I thought was really important was the support that came from our Superintendent, Carolyn Getridge, and the school board members, especially Toni Cook. They really took a bold stand in the cause for African-American education.

The downside of the debate is that there were African Americans who were so ashamed, so afraid, and so paranoid about what we were doing in Oakland. I don't blame the media for this. My job is to teach and the media's job is to sensationalize news. But I do blame those of us who picked up for the media and helped them do their job.

It bothered me that in 1997, scholarly African Americans did not tell the media, "Let me take the time to go to the source and talk to someone in Oakland before I talk to you." That bothered me more than anything.

An Ante-Bellum Sermon

PAUL LAURENCE DUNBAR

We is gathahed hyeah, my brothahs,
     In dis howlin' wildaness,
Fu' to speak some words of comfo't
     To each othah in distress.
An' we chooses fu' ouah subjic'
     Dis — we'll 'splain it by an' by;
"An' de Lawd said, 'Moses, Moses,'
     An' de man said, 'Hyeah am I.'"

Now ole Pher'oh, down in Egypt,
     Was de wuss man evah bo'n,
An' he had de Hebrew chillun
     Down dah wukin' in his co'n;
'T well de Lawd got tiahed o' his foolin',
     An' sez he: "I'll let him know —
Look hyeah, Moses, go tell Pher'oh
     Fu' to let dem chillun go."

"An' ef he refuse to do it,
     I will make him rue de houah,
Fu' I'll empty down on Egypt
     All de vials of my powah."

Yes, he did — an' Pher'oh's ahmy
            Was n't wuth a ha'f a dime;
Fu' de Lawd will he'p his chillun,
            You kin trust him evah time.

An' yo' enemies may 'sail you
            In de back an' in de front;
But de Lawd is all aroun' you,
            Fu' to ba' de battle's brunt.
Dey kin fo'ge yo' chains an' shackles
            F'om de mountains to de sea;
But de Lawd will sen' some Moses
            Fu' to set his chillun free.

An' de lan' shall hyeah his thundah,
            Lak a blas' f'om Gab'el's ho'n,
Fu' de Lawd of hosts is mighty
            When he girds his ahmor on.
Bu fu' feah some one mistakes me,
            I will pause right hyeah to say,
Dat I'm still a-preachin' ancient,
            I ain't talkin' 'bout to-day.

But I tell you, fellah christuns,
            Things'll happen mighty strange;
Now, de Lawd done dis fu' Isrul,
            An' his ways don't nevah change,
An' de love he showed to Isrul
            Was n't all on Isrul spent;
Now don't run an' tell yo' mastahs
            Dat I's preachin' discontent.

'Cause I is n't; I'se a-judgin'
      Bible people by deir ac's;
I'se a-givin' you de Scriptuah,
      I'se a-handin' you de fac's.
Cose ole Pher'oh b'lieved in slav'ry,
      But de Lawd he let him see,
Dat de people he put bref in, —
      Evah mothah's son was free.

An' dahs othahs thinks lak Pher'oh,
      But dey calls de Scriptuah liar,
Fu' de Bible says "a servant
      Is a-worthy of his hire."
An' you cain't git roun' nor thoo dat,
      An' you cain't git ovah it,
Fu' whatevah place you git in,
      Dis hyeah Bible too'll fit.

So you see de Lawd's intention,
      Evah sence de worl' began,
Was dat His almighty freedom
      Should belong to evah man,
But I think it would be bettah,
      Ef I'd pause agin to say,
Dat I'm talkin' 'bout ouah freedom
      In a Bibleistic way.

But de Moses is a-comin',
      An' he's comin', suah and fas'
We kin hyeah his feet a-trompin',
      We kin hyeah his trumpit blas'.

But I want to wa'n you people,
        Don't you git too brigity;
An' don't you git to braggin'
        'Bout dese things, you wait an' see.

But when Moses wif his powah
        Comes an' sets us chillun free,
We will praise de gracious Mastah
        Dat has gin us liberty;
An' we'll shout ouah halleluyahs,
        On dat mighty reck'nin' day,
When we'se reco'nised ez citiz' —
        Huh uh! Chillun, let us pray!

The Seedling

PAUL LAURENCE DUNBAR

As a quiet little seedling
      Lay within its darksome bed,
To itself it fell a-talking,
      And this is what it said:

"I am not so very robust,
      But I'll do the best I can;"
And the seedling from that moment
      Its work of life began.

So it pushed a little leaflet
      Up into the light of day,
To examine the surroundings
      And show the rest the way.

The leaflet liked the prospect,
      So it called its brother, Stem;
Then two other leaflets heard it,
      And quickly followed them.

Rend not the oak and the ivy in twain,
Nor the swart maid from her swarthier swain.

Kitchen Poets and Classroom Books:
Literature from Children's Roots

TERRY
MEIER

Among the many colorful examples of children's work hanging on the walls outside Ilene Carver's second grade classroom in Boston last year was a crayon portrait of two African-American heroines, Harriet Tubman and Rosa Parks. The seven-year-old artist had titled her portrait "Sisters for Freedom." Although over a hundred years of history separated the lives of these two women, in DeKasha's portrait they appear side by side, united in common struggle. At the end-of-the-year assembly several months later, DeKasha stood in front of the school community and proudly declared her intention of becoming a "freedom fighter" when she grew up.

DeKasha's portrait and the words she spoke at the assembly are a powerful testament to the success of Carver's second grade literacy curriculum because they illustrate how for DeKasha, as well as for the other children in Carver's classroom, books became connected to real life. In terms of children's literacy development, nothing is more important than this connection. In his autobiography, Malcolm X tells us that even though he already knew how to read and write when he went to prison, it was only when he discovered, in the prison library, books that presented the real history of Black people that he truly became literate. Similarly, the novelist Paule Marshall (1983) writes of her own early literacy that even though she spent many hours in the Macon Street library reading "voraciously" from the works of European and Euro-American writers, she always sensed that something she couldn't quite define was missing until, one day, as she writes:

> [B]rowsing in the poetry section, I came across a book by someone called Paul Laurence Dunbar, and opening it, I found the photograph of a wistful, sad-eyed poet who to my surprise was black. I turned to a poem at random. "Little brown baby wif spa'klin-eyes — come to yo' pappy an' set on his knee." Although I had a little difficulty at first with the words in dialect, the poem spoke to me as nothing I had read before of the closeness, the special relationship, I had had with my father ... And I began to search then for books and stories and poems about the "race" (as it was put back then), about my people. (p. 10)

The little girl narrator of Ntozake Shange's poem "toussaint" (1975) describes how she snuck into the adult reading room of the St. Louis Public Library and discovered a book about the Haitian revolutionary leader, Toussaint L'Ouverture. Like DeKasha, who made a connection between her own life and the long-ago lives of two women she knew only through text, Shange's narrator transforms the "dead Toussaint" into an imaginative presen(t)ce:

> *Toussaint L'Ouverture*
> *waz the beginnin of reality for me*
> *in the summer contest for*
> *who colored child can read*
> *15 books in three weeks*
> *i won & raved abt TOUSSAINT*
> *L'OUVERTURE*
> *at the afternoon ceremony*
> *waz disqualified*
>   *cuz Toussaint*
>   *belonged in the ADULT*
> *READING ROOM*

& i cried
& carried dead Toussaint home in
the book
he waz dead & livin to me (pp. 26–27)

Many teachers today recognize how important it is for children to see themselves — their experiences, their cultural traditions, their histories — reflected in the literature that is read and discussed in the classroom. For example, while Shange's eight-year-old narrator — circa 1954 — had to invade the adult reading room of the public library in order to discover a book about Toussaint L'Ouverture, children in Monique Brinson's classroom in Boston can find a children's book about him on the shelves of their own classroom library. Fortunately, there are an increasing number of classrooms like Brinson's and Carver's (though not nearly enough) where African-American children not only learn about people and events important in and to their history, but also read many books written by African-American authors. These books present children with a rich variety of real and imagined situations, characters, and themes that reflect the diversity of African-American experience and that help make the act of literacy meaningful to children's lives.

LANGUAGE MODELS

Books written by African-American authors are important to children's literacy development for another reason as well. Many of these writers draw on the stylistic and rhetorical features of African-American oral and literary traditions. In doing so, they provide powerful linguistic models for children to draw on in developing their own speaking and writing abilities. The importance of such models for young writers and speakers cannot be overestimated.

In an essay entitled "The Poets in the Kitchen," Paule Marshall (1983) traces the earliest and most significant influence on her writing back to the basement kitchen of the brownstone house where she grew up and where her mother and her friends, exhausted from cleaning white people's houses all day, would gather around the kitchen table for tea, cocoa, and conversation in the late afternoons. Reflecting back on the importance of those conversations for her later development as a writer, Marshall writes:

> For me, sitting over in the corner, being seen but not heard, which was the rule for children in those days, it wasn't only what the women talked about — the content — but the way they put things — their style. The insight, irony, wit and humor they brought to their stories and discussions and their poet's inventiveness and daring with language. . . . (pp. 7–8)

The importance of stylistic models — that is, ways of *using* language — that resonate with the developing writer's own linguistic and cultural experiences is echoed by the literary scholar Henry Louis Gates, Jr. (1990), when he describes his adolescent encounter with the work of James Baldwin. While Marshall describes features of oral language, in the passage below Gates focuses on an example drawn from the Black literary tradition:

> Finding James Baldwin and writing him down at an Episcopal church camp during the Watts riots in 1965 (I was fifteen) probably determined the direction of my intellectual life more than any other single factor. I wrote and rewrote verbatim his elegantly framed paragraphs, full of sentences that were somehow Henry Jamesian and King Jamesian, yet clothed in the cadences and figures of the spirituals. . . . (p. 58)

The connection Gates makes between discovering the power and beauty of Baldwin's language and the subsequent course of his intellectual life speaks not only to the close relationship between language and identity, but suggests as well the intimate connection between *what* is said and *how* it is said, between meaning and the language that encodes it. Geneva

Smitherman (1973), for example, makes the point that although the Black Language sentence "God don' never change" and the Standard English sentence "God doesn't ever change" may appear at a superficial level to be near-equivalents, in terms of the deeper meanings they convey, they are in reality worlds apart. The second sentence cannot replace the first without significant loss of meaning (despite how glibly teachers sometimes talk with students about "translating" their language into "Standard English").

Significantly, when asked by an interviewer what she thought made her writing so distinctive, the Nobel Prize winner Toni Morrison responded by talking about Black Language:

> The language, only the language. . . . It's the thing black people love so much — the saying of words, holding them on the tongue, experimenting with them, playing with them. It's a love, a passion. Its function is like a preacher's: to make you stand up out of your seat, make you lose yourself and hear yourself. The worst of all possible things that could happen would be to lose that language. There are certain things I cannot say without recourse to my language. (LeClair, 1981, p. 27)

As teachers, what Morrison says about Black Language should give us great pause. "The worst of all possible things that could happen would be to lose that language," she tells us. What do Morrison's words mean for teachers who work with African-American students, especially African-American students who speak Black Language/Ebonics as their first language?

Most fundamentally, I think Morrison's words suggest that as teachers we have a responsibility not to destroy with one hand what we are ostensibly trying to nurture with the other. Her words caution us not to embrace so narrow a conception of literacy — so narrow a conception of what it means to be an effective writer, a powerful speaker — that we end up choking off children's linguistic roots, turning their language(s) into what bell hooks calls "outlawed tongues, renegade speech," denying legitimacy to the very linguistic abilities children need to draw on in order to become what Malcolm X would term truly literate.

STANDARD BLACK ENGLISH

Does this mean that because access to one's native language variety is so important, we don't really need to insist that all students master the standard code? Of course not. Proficiency in the standard code is essential to survival in the United States. But using the standard code does *not* mean that students have to give up all the stylistic and rhetorical features associated with Black Language/Ebonics. Shirley Lewis (1981), for example, describes a highly successful writing program for community college students that is based on the notion of helping students acquire competence in what Lewis terms "Standard Black English." While proficiency in Standard Black English requires that speakers and writers conform to the grammatical conventions of the standard code, it allows for the incorporation of many stylistic features associated with Black oral and written traditions — for example, characteristic intonational patterns; metaphorical language; concrete examples and analogies to make a point; rhyme, rhythm, alliteration, and other forms of repetition, including word play; use of proverbs, aphorisms, biblical quotations, and learned allusions; colorful and unusual vocabulary; arguing *to* a main point (rather than *from* a main point); making a point through indirection.

The concept of Standard Black English is potentially powerful for students at all grade levels, especially for speakers of Black English/Ebonics. It establishes a standard of excellence that incorporates not only features of language they are likely to hear in their own homes and communities, but also features of language characteristic of the rich African-American oral and literary traditions that are these children's rightful legacy.

Many educators lament the fact that some African-American students seem to reject literacy and, in Franz Fanon's terms, to equate "talk(ing) like a book" with "talk(ing) like a white man." To the extent that this equation holds true in the experience of African-American children, we need to ask ourselves what we are doing (or not doing) in our classrooms that lends credence to this false equation. Over their twelve years of elementary and secondary schooling, for example, how many African-American students get the opportunity to read a sizeable portion of the vast body of literature written by African-American authors, the opportunity to discover for themselves that — if number and quality of books, articles, poems, and plays written by African Americans over the last two centuries are the measure — then in fact there *is* no contradiction between "book talk" and "Black talk"?

As teachers, one of our most important responsibilities toward African-American children (and indeed, toward all children) is to insure that they gain exposure to this literature and that they are provided opportunities to respond to and reflect upon it through multiple mediums (for example, writing, discussion, art, music, drama) and in multiple ways, including using this literature as sources of stylistic inspiration for their own experimentations with language.

METALINGUISTIC AWARENESS

As with adult literature, the children's literature written by African Americans reflects the diversity of language varieties represented in African-American communities. A number of very talented contemporary writers incorporate features of Black Language/Ebonics in their books. In addition to their general literary merit, such books are particularly useful for talking with children about linguistic diversity and for helping them to develop more conscious awareness of how they (and others) use language, what sociolinguists and others refer to as *metalinguistic awareness*. This is an extremely important part of literacy instruction because as children increase their metalinguistic awareness, they gain greater facility in adjusting their linguistic strategies to accomplish different purposes and to suit different audiences.

Flossie and the Fox, by Patricia McKissack, is an excellent example of a book that could be used very effectively to increase children's metalinguistic understandings. Set in rural Tennessee, probably sometime in the early 1900s, the book tells the story of a little girl named Flossie who is able to outwit a fox by pretending not to believe he's really a fox. While the fox speaks in standard code, Flossie, her grandmother and the narrator all use linguistic features that McKissack identifies in her "Author's Note" as characteristic of "the rich and colorful dialect of the rural South."

Flossie not only uses her superior reasoning ability to outwit Fox; she also uses language more effectively than he does. In a manner akin to "signifyin(g)" in African-American vernacular and literary traditions, Flossie subverts Fox's potential power by turning his own pompous language against him. By skillfully playing off his words, Flossie exposes Fox's "sense" as nonsense. For example, when Fox tells her " 'I am a fox, and you will act accordingly,' " the indomitable Flossie responds, " 'Unless you can show you a fox, I'll not accord you nothing.' " By the end of the story, Fox has been reduced to following behind Flossie, "begging to be believed," and Flossie has been able to arrive at her destination safe from harm.

USING FLOSSIE AND THE FOX

There are a number of ways that teachers can use *Flossie and the Fox* to increase the linguistic awareness of children. Following are some possibilities.

Activity: Writing Like a Fox

Purposes: To develop a vocabulary for describing different language styles. To identify specific features associated with using the standard code. To practice using those features in a highly conscious way.

Note: Depending on your class's level of independence in writing, you may decide to have children work on this activity individually, in small groups, or as a whole-class writing project.

Procedure: Assign children the task of writing about the events that occurred in the story from Fox's perspective. Imagine, for instance, that Fox is writing a letter to a friend or relative. Explain to the class how important it is to make sure the letter "sounds like Fox." Tell the class that you are going to read the book aloud again and that you want them to listen very carefully to how Fox talks. How is his language different from Flossie's? Write characteristic samples of his speech on chart paper or the board. Help children focus on specific features like vocabulary, sentence length, word endings. When writing is done, have children read letters (or class letter) aloud. Encourage dramatic reading. Analyze results. Discuss process.

Possible Extensions: (1) focus children's conscious attention on their own code-switching abilities by having children spontaneously role- play different social situations. While children are performing, classmates should be taking "notes" about specific features of language they hear changing. (2) Invite guest speakers, bilingual and not, who will talk about the way they vary their language in different situations and why. (3) Assign students to listen for specific language features on the radio and on television. (4) Have children role-play reversing language styles for Flossie and Fox.

Activity: Using Your Words

Purposes: To focus attention on stylistic and rhetorical elements of language. To identify specific features of Flossie's language that enable her to outwit the fox. To practice using language in ways that help resolve conflicts in "peaceable" ways.

Procedure: Have a discussion with children about Flossie's ability to handle conflict by using words effectively (something teachers are always urging them to do). Ask children to think about what specific aspects of language help her do this. Read the story again with a focus on analyzing Flossie's style. Write the examples on chart paper or the board and discuss. Help children focus on specifics (using logical arguments, making analogies, using word play and humor, getting to point). Contrast this with Fox's style. Have children role-play various conflict situations that occur in school and on the playground, one child imitating Fox's style while another tries to imitate Flossie's.

Possible Extensions: (1) Encourage children to bring in examples of effective or clever uses of language that they observe in their neighborhood, at home, on TV, and so forth. (2) Put some of children's favorite "Flossie quotations" on poster board and incorporate them into classroom conversation where appropriate. (3) Incorporate Flossie and her style as a "rhetorical model" in the classroom — for example, when appropriate ask, "What do you think Flossie might say or do in this situation?" (4) As a class project (or in groups), create new Flossie stories where she talks her way out of difficult situations.

Activity: "Sounding" Word Endings

Purposes: To focus attention on alternate pronunciations that potentially could cause confusion in reading and writing instruction. To increase facility in "hearing" and producing various styles of speech.

Procedure: Help children notice that one difference between Fox's language and the language used by Flossie, Big Mama, and the narrator is in the way certain words are pronounced. For this activity, focus children's attention on word endings. Contrast examples from the book (for example, Fox says "child" and "top of the morning" while Flossie says "chile" and "heap o' words"; the narrator says that Fox was "sittin'" and "expectin' somebody"). Facilitate discussion about variation in pronunciation of word endings and its relationship to social context, degree of formality, and so forth. (Point out variation in single speaker's language — for example, the narrator sometimes "sounds" final *ng* and sometimes not.) Have children "play" with these different sounds, individually and in chorus. Talk about McKissack's use of the apostrophe and her efforts to capture in writing the way people actually sound when they speak. Read or write on board samples of Flossie's and narrator's speech in which McKissack uses an apostrophe to indicate "missing letters." Have children "translate" into standard spelling.

Possible Extensions: (1) Create various scripts for children to use in role-playing (these should emphasize word endings). Have children dramatize these scripts, one time in the "voice" of a very formal speaker and again in the "voice" of a speaker using language more informally. Have children exaggerate the sounds of word endings when speaking in the formal voice. (2) Make up fun sentences. Read to children with final "sounds" unvoiced. Have children "translate" those words into standard spelling. (3) Have children listen to voices on radio and record ending sounds they hear. (4) When appropriate during reading lessons or other literacy activities, invite children to read "like Fox," exaggerating sounds of word endings (*s*, *ng*, and so forth).

"Listen to Your Students": An Interview with Oakland High School English Teacher Hafeezah AdamaDavia Dalji

Following is an interview with Hafeezah Adama-Davia Dalji, a high school English teacher in the Oakland public schools. Dalji was the first African-American woman to head the English Department at Castlemont, one of the largest high schools in Oakland. She is also national vice president of the National Association of Black Reading and Language Development. Dalji was interviewed by Barbara Miner, managing editor of *Rethinking Schools*.

Can you explain your background as a teacher and how you became involved in the Standard English Proficiency program (SEP) in Oakland?

I have been teaching with the Oakland public school system since 1973. Right now I am at Castlemont High School, teaching sophomore and junior English. I have approximately 160 students in five classes; about 30 of them are Spanish-speaking students, about 5 are East Asian or Vietnamese, and the rest are African students. I like to say "African" students because we are here in America, and I don't feel I have to say African-American to refer to those African students who were born in an American diaspora. I also have some autonomous African students, that is, students born in Africa, and I don't want them to feel left out. I don't have any European, that is, white, students in my class.

There has been a SEP program in Oakland for a number of years but until about four years ago, to my knowledge the extent of the program was a yearly event held at the Hilton or some other hotel. Today, the SEP program has at least begun to scratch the surface, due to a group of dedicated, committed and competent African and African-oriented teachers in the district. My interest in the SEP program is that it is a vehicle to address the specific needs of African students in Oakland. As an educator, I have always understood that as long as African students respond to and accept, without question, European reality, they will never be able to see, think, feel and act in a fashion that affirms and protects their being.

Can you give one example of how an African cultural perspective affects your classroom practice?

When students enter the classroom, there is a beautiful mural with drawings that represent the African Maat symbols, based on ancient Egyptian/African culture. There are seven symbols: righteousness, truth, honesty, propriety, harmony, order, and reciprocity. Last year, one of my students drew a symbol of reciprocity — hands on top of each other exchanging fruit, one giving and one taking. The symbol is beautifully drawn, with wonderful colors of orange, black, brown, and green. Another Maat principle, harmony, is drawn from an Asian perspective. That is, the symbol is the yin and yang — one big circle broken into half, evenly balanced and in colors of black and white. Also, the symbol of justice, in the form of a scale that is evenly balanced, is drawn over the entrance of the door. I also have on the ceiling — and I began this early in my teaching career, to use the ceiling — we have symbols of the seven Kwaanza concepts. These are, first in Swahili then in English, Umoja (unity), Kujichagulia (self-determination), Ujima (collective work and responsibility), Ujamaa (cooperative economics), Nia (purpose), Kuumba (creativity), and Imani (faith). The word *Ebonics*, that is, the language that the masses of African people speak, regardless of the diaspora, is also located on the ceiling, with explanations and examples.

I believe that academic development, skills development, and character development all go together. Character development is very much a part of my lesson plan. So in the beginning of the year, we talk about what the symbols mean and how we are going to use them in our English curriculum. For example, as we go through literature the students will identify and describe a character of integrity, propriety, truth, honesty and so on. I use these ancient African symbols to help develop character in not only the African students but all students. What is good for African students and what works for them is good for all students. One of my favorite sayings is the quote, "Education is a combination of high academic skills, with high moral, social and spiritual values, propelled by common sense."

How do you begin the school year?

Teachers have to provide or manufacture a way for students to be successful in the beginning. One of my favorite sayings, for instance, is: "Outside the classroom the student must live in the world; inside the classroom the student must own the world." So I begin the year by asking the students to write short descriptive vignettes, after first studying models of vignettes written by previous students.

I have them write eleven different vignettes on categories such as, what is your name? For example, what is its cultural meaning? What does your name mean to you, or who you are named after? Then I have them do other vignettes. Maybe it will be about something they accomplished that made them feel great, or one of their most embarrassing incidents and how it was solved, or something they struggled to overcome or change about themselves, or an event that made them proud of their culture, heritage, and race, or a family experience that influenced them in a powerful way. When the vignettes are done, I teach them how to put those paragraphs together and how to use transitions. By the end, all the students have an autobiography. Everybody is successful. I have students who told me, "I can't write." And I would say, "Oh yes you can." Sentence by sentence, paragraph by paragraph, they build an autobiography from short vignettes. Students who thought they couldn't even write a sentence write page after page.

In African/American-African culture, a celebration culminates each successful passage. So after a successful unit, students plan a sharing event. Parents and other community leaders will be invited, and there will be food, dancing and so on. And these students will literally hunger for another success, and another, and another. From this activity the students learn the truth of the African proverb, "The stick to save you is found in your hands."

What are some of the books you use in your English class?

We have several anthologies we are studying from. One is a book with African-American literature, and we are currently using the unit on folklore. I also have anthologies with Mexican-American literature and of course I have the European-American literature. Most of all, I believe it is important to remember that literature is not literature if students cannot relate it to their lives.

In addition to the poetry, and stories, and other readings in the anthology, we are going to read at least three novels in my junior English class. Some of the favorite novels I have used in past years are *Black Boy* or *Eight Black Men* by Richard Wright, and *Beloved* by Toni Morrison. Actually I use a lot of Toni Morrison and Alice Walker's novels, and I use Naim Ackbar's *Vision of Men*. The students and I also love *Swimming to the Top of the Rain*, by Jay California Cooper. It's a perfect story that shows important lessons about unity and growing up together in a family with lots of siblings. But it is also a story where you can translate every other paragraph from Ebonics to Standard English.

This is what I love about African and African-American writers. They write in Ebonics and Standard English, so students learn to translate the Ebonics to Standard English and the Standard English to Ebonics. They learn too that the African language is beautiful and that no language is superior or inferior. Language is just a vehicle for you to learn and get around in your environment and to express yourself. My students learn that there are certain things written and expressed better in Ebonics than English, and others that are better in English, depending on what you are trying to express. I do this in poetry, too. For example, the poem "I Am" was written by a student of mine several years ago, Le James Riggins.

> *I am a young man.*
> *I am in diaspora.*
> *I am a student.*
> *I am a brother*
> *Trying to survive in the ghetto,*
> *I am an African.*

I be tall.
I be intelligent.
I be fast.
I be calm.
What do you be?

When I have them translate it into Standard English — and the "I be tall" becomes "I am tall" and the "I be intelligent" becomes "I am intelligent" — the students say, "Hey, that doesn't sound right in Standard English."

And here's another one, by my former student Rauf Al-Sabar, "I Am What I Be."

Im a
Black man
With positive dreams.

Im a pocket
Full of ideas
Bursting at the seams.

Im a native
Of this land
But do not care.

Im the same
As you
Breathing the same air.

I be
The man you
Thought was a black sheep.

I be
The host of dream
Visiting in your sleep.

I be
Smart getting
All good grades.

I be
All black
100% African made.

And then I have them translate this poem into Standard English. "Oh no," my students say, "but it doesn't sound right. It messes everything up." So these are vehicles I use to illustrate to students that no language is inferior nor is any language superior.

What does a typical week look like in your class?

On Monday morning we have libations. We have survived a weekend and we have tried to be the best that we can be in all ways through that weekend. In order to be the best that we can be during the rest of the week, we bring the spirits of our ancestors into the room. So we get in a circle and begin libations, remembering an ancestor's name in sharing, and remembering what he or she did. Then we pour water over a plant, so their spirits will continue to grow and flourish within the descendants. The name-calling continues until every student participates. They come to understand that it is an African cultural custom to recognize the deceased on whose shoulders they stand and who will help them get through the week.

After a weekend, the libations help center the students and reintroduce them to the school environment. Class periods are forty-five minutes and sometimes that takes up the entire morning. It depends on what happened in the weekend. These are youngsters in an urban district, and there are a lot of things that might have happened on the weekend, some good and some not so good.

On Tuesday, we either begin a new unit of study or take up where we left off. Right now, one of my classes has begun a unit on folktales, so we are talking about Stagolee, an African-American folk hero. He is the folk hero that nobody could control. Even the "Angel of Death" couldn't control him. He even died when he wanted to die. When the sheriff tried to hang him, his neck wouldn't crack. They kept the rope around his neck for half an hour and still his neck didn't crack. If the people who made the rules said there was no drinking after 12 o'clock, that's when Stagolee would decide to drink.

Folk heroes from other cultures are also studied. From the Latin culture, for example, there are the tales of La Llorona. Folk heroes are universal. One of the ways you hand down culture is through folktales. Those folktales are the lies your mother told you, and then you find out they aren't lies but one of the ways that people raise their children and transfer culture, values, customs, and traditions.

Also on Tuesday, at the beginning of this unit, we might talk about what folktales are, and how they are used, and how they are universal. And we might even do some folk songs. Then we will go over some of the vocabulary and the phrases within Stagolee or the other folktales. This is also another time when I take my Ebonics-speaking students and make them aware of the Standard English speech that we are learning about so that they equate the learning of mainstream Standard English with making money and understanding Europeans in America. So one of the times when I try to move my Ebonics-speaking students to Standard English is when I am preparing them for another unit. I want them to think in both languages, just like the Spanish-speaking students think in both. And for my Spanish-speaking students, I have them translate and practice their language. And I do the same with my Vietnamese students.

How does Wednesday unfold?

After the introduction of a unit, we would begin reading the unit. This is either on Tuesday or Wednesday, depending on the week. I ask for volunteers and we read the story as a class. And we really get into it and select characters. Somebody gets to be Stagolee, somebody is the sheriff, and we get into the drama of the folktale. Interspersed with this are writing assignments. I get to see how the students are understanding the story and how they are understanding different words. The students write in logs — I call them logs instead of diaries and journals — and they write down their ideas, their responses to the story, and what they are learning. When I have them write in class, I get a chance to know what they are understanding in grammar.

For example, presently we are studying rules regarding the comma, and you know there are a lot of rules for the comma. We'll go see how writers use the commas within the book. I have noticed that the comma is one area we really need to study. And that is sometimes part of their quiz: to explain how the comma is used in paragraph two or three. I integrate my grammar into literature-based English. In that way, the students understand how the grammar and the mechanics and everything else related to the English language is used by the authors.

I should also underscore that my students do daily writing. Usually they write in their log book while I take roll. Some of the times they share. At the end of the week I check their logs. Sometimes what they have written is personal. They have to date their logs, but if they write that it is personal, I don't invade their privacy. I just note that they are keeping up with the assignments. If they ask me to read it, I do. But if I am not asked, I don't. I respect their privacy.

And Thursday and Friday?

We've been reading on Tuesday and Wednesday and by Thursday we are probably on our way to ending a story involving Stagolee. We begin studying the characters, and the environment that the characters are in, and how did the environment influence the characters. And we talk about the moral and ethical values regarding the character Stagolee and ask, "Why this reading?" "What are you supposed to learn besides writing and grammar and all of the other English components?" On Friday, sometimes there are quizzes or tests. Sometimes on Friday, I take the students out to different parts of the campus. There is always something they can describe, practicing their descriptive writing and seeing how authors create a setting and environment for their characters. In general, Friday is more of a creative day.

Can you talk more about how you integrate grammar into literature-based lessons?

We are studying the comma now. We have a grammar book and we go over all the rules in that unit on the comma. We will take maybe twenty minutes are so. Then we go back to the novel or short story we are reading and see how the comma is used in the story. So I teach the grammar and literature separately and then I intersperse it so the students can see how the comma and other mechanics are used in the literature they are reading. We also do a lot on semicolons. I love the difference between the dashes and the hyphens. The African students use lots of metaphors. We are always interrupting a sentence, you know, with a nonessential phrase or something because we can't just leave the thought, you just had to be there. So they have to know the difference between the dashes and the hyphens, and they have to understand how to use the comma with nonessential phrases or clauses. The comma is the most complex because there are so many more rules. When I ask them to identify, or rather describe, how a comma is used, I tell them to give me the rule regarding how that comma is used in that particular paragraph. So that means they have to memorize the rules.

Do you use handouts on Ebonics? Or do you do work more organically out of the literature you are using?

I work from the literature that I am reading, although I do use specific Ebonics handouts. I do a combination, actually, several combinations.

Where did you get the handouts?

I make my own handouts on Ebonics. Some of them come from the literature we are reading and some come from listening to my students. My students are the best source for handouts. I usually get more information from them than I can from a premade worksheet, because they come in using the language that they use all the time. And then of course they get excited when they know I get certain language from them and then I show how a writer uses the same language in a book. That lets them know that they are as important as anyone else.

Poetry is very important too. I intersperse poetry and I use it as a preliminary to most of the things that we do. In that way, my students get a chance to recognize the difference ways to use language in poetry, when to use Standard English and when to use Ebonics. I use the poetry that my students write, along with other poetry. I have actual poets come to my class and work with the students. They are better than I am in that particular area and they can get the most out of the students. That is why I get such beautiful poems, because I have these professionals work my students. And, of course, when I can't get the professionals, I can still motivate my students to create beautiful, relevant poetry of all types.

Do you have any specific advice for new teachers?

For one thing, I hate the citizenship grades. In our schools there is both an academic grade in each subject and a citizenship grade. I give a grade in citizenship, but everybody gets an A. Students are growing and I don't use citizenship grades as a means of discipline. My classroom is a family and whatever problems occur there, we settle within the family. Except in extreme circumstances, and with a student who may have severe emotional problems, I don't call the security guards.

Another thing. There must always be character development along with academic development. Also, you can't teach students if you don't care about them. You have to acknowledge and respect their cultural experiences, the knowledge and opinions that they bring to the classroom. As far as curriculum, I would say to new teachers that the curriculum must be demanding and challenging. Our students are not babies and they don't like to be treated like babies and they know when they are being treated like babies.

Do you have any advice specifically for a white teacher in terms of teaching Ebonics-speaking students?

Respect the language of the students. Let them know that no language is inferior nor superior. Give them examples. And of course you have to feel that way, too, because if you don't, there is no sense in trying to teach what you don't feel, because students will see it. You also have to be knowledgeable about Ebonics before you are able to work with students in transferring their language to Standard English. The language is a retention of the West and Niger–Congo African linguistic structure. Ebonics is a beautiful African and Pan-African language of whose metaphorical rhythms and patterns are copied among other racial and cultural groups all over the world.

A European teacher has to recognize that there is a rhythm to the language, they have to recognize the cadence in the language, they have to recognize the rich metaphors, so they can draw upon this when they are trying to tell their students, "Now let's say this is another way, in Standard English."

How might a white teacher learn more about Ebonics?

Listen to the students. Stay in your room at lunch and let the students hang out. You will learn a lot about the language, social interaction, and rules among the students, and who the leaders are among the students. You will also learn about the community. Too many European teachers hang out in the cafeteria with other teachers. When I see a new teacher do that I say to myself, "They're not going to be successful." Also, hang out at school in the afternoon. Let the students know you will be there for them to answer questions or to talk. Don't beat the students to the door. You must be connected to the school community or you will not be a successful educator. You must "bond" with your students, because by knowing them you will become aware of their needs. If you take the time to recognize the cultural and linguistic clues embedded in the body language of African students, students will teach you how to teach them.

Let the blare of Negro Jazz and the bellowing voice of Bessie Smith singing Blues penetrate the closed ears of the colored near-intellectuals until they listen and perhaps understand. Let Paul Robeson singing "Water Boy," and Rudolph Fisher writing about the streets of Harlem, and Jean Toomer holding the heart of Georgia in his hands, and Aaron Douglas drawing strange black fantasies cause the smug Negro middle class to turn from their white, respectable, ordinary books and papers to catch a glimpse of their own beauty. We younger Negro artists who create now intend to express our individual dark-skinned selves without fear or shame. If white people are pleased, we are glad. If they are not, it doesn't matter. We know we are beautiful. And ugly too. The tom-tom cries and the tom-tom laughs. If colored people are pleased we are glad. If they are not, their displeasure doesn't matter either. We build our temples for tomorrow, we know how, and we stand on top of the mountain, free within ourselves.

Langston Hughes
The Nation, *1926*

Teaching Teachers about Black Communications

TERRY
MEIER

In a graduate course I teach at Wheelock College entitled Language and Culture, I typically ask students to analyze a hypothetical interaction between a young student who is presumably a speaker of Black Language/Ebonics and her presumably Standard English-speaking teacher. In this interaction, the student attempts to tell her teacher a story about something she has done over the weekend. The student's initial excitement about sharing her experience with the teacher soon fades into silence, however, when the teacher repeatedly interrupts her story to "correct" both the child's grammar and her pronunciation of certain words.

Most of the students in my classes are either teachers or soon-to-be teachers, and so this exercise is usually the catalyst for a lively discussion about teachers' attitudes towards different language varieties as well as about what the teacher's role should be in helping students acquire skills in the standard code. Not surprisingly, my students are critical of this hypothetical teacher's lack of sensitivity towards her student's feelings as well as her preoccupation with form rather than substance (that is, it's not what this child says the teacher cares about, but only how she says it). Many students also question this teacher's methodology.

Interestingly, however, none of the students ever argues that this teacher shouldn't be trying to teach her students to master Standard English. Through their course readings, students have learned that as a linguistic system, Black Language/Ebonics possesses every bit as much consistency and legitimacy as Standard English. But this academic knowledge does not negate their real-world (and in some cases, very hard-earned) understanding that mastery of Standard English conventions is necessary (though not of course sufficient) for entry into the mainstream professional world.

By the end of our discussion, everyone usually pretty much agrees that the teacher's aim in working with students who speak a language variety other than Standard English is neither to abdicate the responsibility for teaching all children standard conventions nor to replace the student's first language. Rather, the goal is to help students add facility in the standard code to the repertoire of language abilities they already possess (what is referred to as the "additive approach" to bilingual/bidialectal education). What is not so apparent or so easily agreed upon by the end of this discussion, however, are the pedagogical strategies for achieving that goal. How do we help children to become bidialectal or bilingual, equally proficient and "at home" in Standard English and in their own native language variety?

I believe that in order to help children become bidialectal or bilingual, teachers must know something about the systematic features of their students' native language. Perhaps the most important understanding I hope my students take from Language and Culture is that to help children develop exemplary abilities in reading and writing, teachers must be able to link instruction to what is already familiar to their students, whether this be Spanish word order, Haitian Creole verb structures, or Black Language/Ebonics pronunciation rules. One of the most fundamental principles of learning is that in order for learning to occur, new knowledge must be connected to old, that none of us can comprehend new information without making sense of it within the context of what we already know.

It is this principle that underlies the Oakland school board's contention that children who speak Black Language/Ebonics will benefit educationally if their teachers possess knowledge about the systematic features of their language. It is this same principle that undergirds the unit on Black Communications I teach as part of Language and Culture. My purpose here is to describe this unit on Black Communications and to talk about the ways in which I believe learning about Black Language/Ebonics helps prepare my students for teaching more effectively in an increasingly diverse world.

SETTING THE CONTEXT

Consonant with Wheelock College's mission to prepare teachers who can serve "all the nation's children," the broad purpose of Language and Culture is to deepen students' understanding of the complex relationships among language, culture, and identity and to have students reflect on the implications of those connections for their current or future work with children in schools. The four or five weeks that we spend on Black Communications function as a kind of case study within the course. Its purpose is both to help students acquire some specific knowledge about Black Language/Ebonics and to serve as a model of the kinds of understandings teachers need to acquire about the linguistic backgrounds of their students.

The students who have taken the course have been mainly teachers and future teachers from Boston and its surrounding communities, an area of the country that represents significant linguistic diversity. The majority of the students in my classes have been white and female, from a variety of social class backgrounds.

Although a large percentage of these students were either currently teaching or planned to teach in multicultural, multilingual settings, most entered the course with little or no knowledge about Black Language/Ebonics. Many also brought with them negative stereotypes about the language, characterizing it in initial class discussions by terms such as "slang," "street talk," "bad English," "wrong," and "not really a language." Significantly, however, when asked to write (anonymously) about what they considered to be the most valuable knowledge they had gained in the course, over 90 percent of the students who have filled out a course evaluation during the past three years mentioned knowledge about Black Language/Ebonics as either the most valuable thing, or one of the most valuable things, they had gained from the course.

Through course readings and discussion, many students in the course develop a new level of respect for the linguistic integrity and power of Black Language/Ebonics and its importance as a foundation in which to help children build new language skills. Although the assignment of specific readings and the content of class discussions varies somewhat from semester to semester, we always focus, in some form or another, on the broad areas described below.

A HISTORICAL PERSPECTIVE

It is difficult to talk about Black Language/Ebonics in a meaningful way without simultaneously talking about racism. Drawing on a wide variety of sources from the fields of literary criticism, cultural studies, and sociology, we begin the unit on Black Communications with an examination of the way in which "Black Language" has historically been characterized in this country as an inferior form of language, a kind of "broken English" reflecting the supposed simplicity and lack of education of its users. We talk about how distortions of Black speech (bearing little, if any, relationship to the speech patterns of actual human beings), have been used throughout U.S. history in literature, minstrel shows, vaudeville, radio, movies, and television to characterize African Americans as either inarticulate and simpleminded or ultra-urbane and highly sexualized.

As we talk about various historical examples of this phenomenon, students easily draw connections to contemporary caricatures of Black Language/Ebonics that surface on television, in the movies, in racist jokes, in casual conversation and — in the wake of the Oakland school board's resolution on Ebonics — on the Internet as well. Through this process of lecture and discussion, students begin to see that popular conceptions of "Black Language" — conceptions that many of them initially share — are in fact more a figment of white racist imagination than a representation of any "Black reality."

It is against this historical and ideological background that students come to understand that Black Language/Ebonics is not only a systematic, rule-governed language variety, every bit as complex and sophisticated as Standard English, but also that there exists a rich African-American oral and written tradition that draws, in part, upon a distinctive set of stylistic and rhetorical features that are as evident in the writings of Frederick Douglass in the 1830s as in the speeches of Malcolm X in the 1960s and in the essays of Toni Morrison in the 1990s. This is not the "Black Language" that my students ever imagined. When they compare its richness and complexity to the simplistic stereotypes they have absorbed from the popular media, they begin to draw the connections between linguistic diversity and racism that sit at the root of society's negative characterizations of Black Language/Ebonics and that have contributed in such significant measure to obscuring the true abilities of countless African-American children in the nation's schools. From this historical and ideological base, we then examine specific features of Black Language/Ebonics.

PHONOLOGY AND GRAMMAR

As numerous studies of language socialization and uses in African-American communities attest, by the time they enter kindergarten, African-American children are likely to have formed a sense of identity and self-efficacy strongly linked to their ability to use oral language in highly sophisticated and stylized ways (see, e.g., Hale-Benson, 1982; Brice Heath, 1983; Goodwin, 1990; Labov, 1972; Taylor & Dorsey-Gaines, 1988; Vernon-Feagans, 1996). From rhyming games to rap songs, from talking their way out of trouble to instigating trouble, many African-American children use language to display their intelligence and their competence in negotiating the world. In their communities, they are applauded for their quick verbal responses, their creative plays on words and sounds, their imaginative improvisations of familiar stories and themes, and their ability to best an "opponent" through superior verbal reasoning.

These linguistic abilities are potentially powerful precursors to literacy, but only if the teacher is aware of their existence. When teachers know little about the native language varieties of their students, the danger is not only that "differences" will be mistaken for "errors" (as when a teacher rejects a child's rhyme or when children's dialectal pronunciations are "corrected" during oral reading), but that linguistic differences will be interpreted by the teacher as evidence of some cognitive difficulty. For example, a child who speaks Black Language/Ebonics as a first language and does not use -s to mark plural nouns (who says, for instance, *ten cent* rather than *ten cents*) is displaying "linguistic behavior" perfectly consistent with the grammatical rules of Black Language/Ebonics, which does not require -s to mark plurality. Not knowing the systematic rules of the child's language, it would be easy for a teacher to arrive at the erroneous conclusion that a child who says *three book* or *two boy* does not possess the concept of plurality. Obviously there is a vast difference between the pedagogical and interactional strategies employed by a teacher who believes that she is working with a child who lacks a concept of plurality and one who realizes that the child is simply unfamiliar or unpracticed with how this concept is coded in Standard English. There is a difference as well in the way the teacher in these two situations is likely to assess the intellectual potential of the child.

Although I do not require that students in my classes memorize a list of phonological and grammatical differences between Black Language/ Ebonics and Standard English, we do read about and discuss these differences in some detail as well as reflect upon their implications for effective teaching practice and for the accurate assessment of African-American children's cognitive and linguistic abilities.

PRAGMATICS

Phonological and grammatical features are only part of what makes up a language. Membership in a particular speech community entails knowledge of a wide range of communicative skills and strategies for acting in the world — for demonstrating intelligence, apologizing, asking for a favor, telling someone what to do, claiming allegiance with others, displaying status, getting one's point across, even telling a story. The way in which people use language to accomplish these and other social actions is referred to as *pragmatics*. People socialized in different cultural communities often utilize very different verbal strategies for performing these actions. As many language researchers have noted, differences in the way language is *used* in various communities frequently cause more communicative misunderstandings in classrooms than do phonological and grammatical differences. For this reason, we spend a good deal of time talking about pragmatic features of language.

With respect to differences between Black Language/Ebonics and Standard English on the level of pragmatics, much research suggests that one of the ways in which children raised in white, mainstream communities learn to display intelligence is by responding correctly to "known answer" questions like, "What is that?"; "How many did you find?"; "Do you remember what tomorrow is?" In contrast, one of the most important ways in which young children in many working-class African-American communities are socialized to display intelligence is by responding in spontaneous and creative ways to verbal challenges issued by an adult or an older child — for example, "What you gonna do, I try to take dis?"; "What's dat like?"; "What you think you are?" (examples from Heath, 1983). A particularly vivid example of a child's creative response to an adult challenge comes from Heath's 1983 study of language socialization in an African-American community she calls Trackton. In this example, Lem, age twenty-eight months, is responding to his mother, Lillie Mae:

> On one occasion, Lillie Mae, exasperated with Lem for taking off his shoes, asked him what he had done with his shoes and suggested: "You want me ta tie you up, put you on de railroad track?" Lem hesitated a moment and responded:
>
> > Railroad track
> > Train all big 'n black
> > On dat track, on dat track,
> > on dat track
> > Ain't no way I can't get back

Back from dat track

Back from dat train

Big 'n black, I be back.

Heath (1983) reports that "everyone laughed uproariously" at Lem's response, and nothing more was said about his missing shoes (p. 110).

These two very different ways of displaying intelligence — in the one case, by giving correct information in response to "known answer" questions, and in the other, by creatively manipulating the sounds and sense of language in response to more open-ended verbal challenges — prepare children in different ways for handling the instructional tasks they confront in the early years of school. Heath (1983) reports, for instance, that many Trackton children were unfamiliar with and puzzled by their teachers' use of "known answer" questions, and the teachers of these children frequently complained that many seemed unable to answer "the simplest kind of questions" (p. 283). Meanwhile, the linguistic abilities for which children had been praised and reinforced in Trackton — creative word play, extensive use of metaphor and simile, the ability to think on one's feet and to adjust language to audience — were not evident in school because, for a variety of reasons, teachers did not provide instructional opportunities that elicted their use.

Ironically, in her study of language socialization at home and in school, Vernon-Feagans (1996) speculates that the working-class African-American kindergartners in the study may have performed less well on a paraphrasing task than their white mainstream counterparts precisely *because* of their more creative use of language and their superior storytelling abilities. Rather than simply retelling the story when asked to paraphrase, the African-American children added and embellished the story and, in the process, "frequently ended up creating a different, but often more interesting, vignette" (p. 198). But although their vignettes were often more interesting than the original, the process of embellishment led the African-American children to exclude elements of the original vignette, for which they were penalized when their performance on the paraphrasing task was evaluated. This is not surprising. Studies consistently show that teachers commonly underestimate or fail to recognize entirely many of the verbal abilities nurtured in African-American communities.

In addition to helping my students become aware of the kinds of linguistic abilities African-American children bring with them to school, we also spend time in the course discussing specific ways in which teachers can draw upon and nurture those abilities during literacy instruction. We examine children's literature that incorporates features of Black Language/Ebonics as well as excerpts from the work of prominent writers and speakers who employ characteristic rhetorical features associated with African-American oral and written traditions. As we discuss in class, such literature provides a context both for celebrating linguistic diversity and for discussing issues like code switching, attitudes about language, and the relationship between language and power — all of which can be appropriate and fascinating topics even for children as young as kindergarten age. Just as importantly, literature that incorporates stylistic features of Black Language/Ebonics can be used as models for children to experiment with the stylistic features of their own writing.

Clearly, our four- or five-week examination of Black Language/Ebonics only scratches the surface of an immensely complex, enormously exciting, and ever-evolving field of study. As I think my students understand by the end of the course, Black Language/Ebonics is not a static, unchanging, monolithic entity. Like all languages, Black Language/Ebonics is multiple — a living, vibrant, constantly changing phenomenon, as multifaceted and multivoiced as the diversity of speakers and writers who sound and re-sound its stylistic continuum. Each semester that I teach Language and Culture, I end in the hope that my students' explorations of the richness and complexity of African-American language and literature are only just beginning.

Ebonics Speakers and Cultural, Linguistic, and Political Test Bias

MARY RHODES HOOVER

The earliest tests were used to sort people. They were developed in the 1920s with support from corporate foundations. They were IQ tests based on the early Army Alpha Test used to assign soldiers to different tasks. They were used to select out individuals having certain values, moralities, and skills (Hoover, Politzer, & Taylor, 1991, p. 92). The same type of sorting goes on with testing today.

The current standards movement, where organizations are attempting to draft national benchmarks (for example, the National Council of Teachers of English and the International Reading Association), and with President Clinton endorsing a national program to test students in reading at the fourth grade level and in math at the eighth grade level, threatens to become yet another occasion for sorting. African Americans have always been concerned about their children having access to the highest quality of education, to the kind of education required for first-class citizenship. This concern for education is clear, from the many African-American independent schools founded since 1865 to the current endorsement of African-American parents of the basics as their first priority for the public schools. Most recently, Bob Moses struggled for ten years in Cambridge, Massachusetts, until the school committee finally voted to make algebra available to all eighth grades. And yet, we are worried about standardization, those testing programs all over this country that will determine who gets a high school diploma, who will matriculate at certain high schools, who will become teachers, and so on.

Testing mandates, with their biases, imposed by various institutions and jurisdictions were already causing Blacks to be "legislated out of education" (Wiley, 1990); there appears to be little attempt to correct these errors on the part of the new standards makers, test creators, or the administrators who purchase them.

In addition to their basic intent to sort people, most tests are also particularly biased against Ebonics speakers and other bilingual/bidialectal/bicultural students. For example, African-American children acquire varying degrees of proficiency in African-American Language (Ebonics) as well as in Standard English. At school, it is generally only their proficiency in Standard English that is tested. This one-sided testing can give the appearance that a child who masters Ebonics much better than Standard English suffers from a general language deficiency. The competency of the African-American student needs to be measured by a variety of tests, and the tests that are given should be examined for cultural, linguistic, psychological, or political bias. Some examples of these biases follow.

An excellent example of cultural/economic bias is the following item: A gentleman has on a suit and he's carrying a briefcase. Black children and white children are both asked, "Where is this gentleman going?" White children will say, "He's going to work." Black children are asked the same question and they say "church. He's dressed in a suit. He's going to church." Both of them are correct. Economically, because 90 percent of Blacks are not white-collar workers, that is a correct answer for the Black child. If he's got on his suit, he's going to church. Yet if a white child says the correct answer is work, the white child would get the IQ score necessary to stay in a regular class and achieve. On the other hand, the Black child who answers "church" would be marked down — each of these items is worth 2 or 3 percent of the total — and perhaps spend the rest of his or her school career in a mentally retarded class, if asked other similarly biased questions (Hoover, Politzer, & Taylor, 1991, p. 82).

Another example of cultural/economic bias is seen in the Law School Admissions Test (LSAT) (White, 1992):

It is often true that children who perform poorly when they begin school have had few toys and no books to aid the development of their minds. The parents of these unfortunate youngsters are remiss in failing to provide their children with these tools of development and therefore, for causing their lack of preparedness for school.

   The author's argument is logically based on which of the following assumptions:

   I. Children supplied with toys and books excel in school.
   II. Parents should know the value of toys and books.
   III. Parents have the means to provide their children with toys and books.

   A. I only
   B. I and II only
   C. I and III only
   D. II and III only
   E. I, II, and III

   D is the correct answer.

This class-tied item asserts that parents are the factor "causing" their children's "lack of preparedness for school," taking a political position in the "Great Debate" over the cause of minority school failure — the parents or the school system. (Most evidence supports the system, e.g., Hoover, Dabney, & Lewis, 1990.)

There's a general cultural and lexical bias in terms of the scene and subject matter of the comprehension and vocabulary sections of many reading tests. For example, on one comprehension subtest students are asked to respond to the following: If a person does something against the law he is: an ambassador, offender, official, or officer. The answer could be either the second or fourth response to someone familiar with the brutality, graft, and corruption characteristic of some police departments (Hoover, Politzer, & Taylor, 1991, p. 90).

An example of linguistic bias is the phonological bias found in the scoring of oral reading tests. In administering these tests, such as the oral assessments in the Ekwall/Shanker Reading Inventory (1993), no directions are given to the teacher in terms of scoring the tests for reading errors and not for speech errors. A reading teacher thus has no guidance on whether to score a student who pronounces *walked* as *walkded* or *with* as *wif*— both dialect-influenced patterns — as correct — if the student comprehends the paragraph — or incorrect.

Another example is the use of tests for the disadvantage of one group and the advantage of others: Many states have literacy tests that penalize the student by issuing him or her a certificate rather than a diploma. Here you have an educational enterprise involving several groups: teachers, administrators, and students. The school fails in one of its endeavors to teach the students literacy skills. Of the groups involved in the failure, one group is singled out for penalty. Not the group that failed to teach in spite of the voluminous research demonstrating how simple it is to teach reading; not the group that failed to administer a successful school program (and again we have voluminous research showing that a principal who knows something about instruction is a basic characteristic of these schools). No, the group singled out to suffer for the failure of schools to educate Blacks is the group which had the least responsibility for the situation — the students (Hoover, Politzer, & Taylor, 1991).

Bias is also present in the various test genres. For example, tests of comprehension are much more subject to bias than tests of vocabulary. The rationale for this difference is that comprehension measurements depend heavily on inference, which is much more culture bound and less objective a measurement than other components of reading such as vocabulary, according to John Carrol (1972). Students from a culture in which inference is often couched in proverbial usage and based on an African-oriented worldview Alleyne (1980) calls "inversion" may not be as familiar with European styles of inference as traditional students.

African-American students generally have higher scores on vocabulary than on comprehension subtests. Yet one of the newest tests, the Terra Nova Test, only assesses comprehension (not vocabulary) and is used as the major testing instrument in a number of districts.

There is general ambiguity in many of the reading tests that would create a problem for most students, but particularly those students who are bilingual or bidialectal, that is, with different languages and dialects in their backgrounds, who understand Standard English, but perhaps not the superstandard English (Fasold, 1972) found on many tests. For example, in a 1983 version of the Florida College Level Academic Skills Test (CLAST) word usage section, which was given to all sophomores who wanted to go on to the junior year, students had to choose the best definition of an *outline* among the following: *essence, major idea, basic essentials*, and *fundamental ingredient*. All of the above could be correct.

In the sentence structure section of the same test, the student was asked to select the correct answer of the best answer among the following:

> A. After falling down the steps, misplacing his mail, and failing his English test, John went to bed.
>
> B. John decided to go to bed because he fell down the steps, misplaced his mail, and failed his English test.

"A" is allegedly the best answer, but both would appear to be correct to a student, however literate, who had learned Standard English as a second language. Yet students would have been penalized and not allowed to go on to the junior year of college in Florida based on such ridiculous items as this.

A final problem is that tests often are not valid. That is, they do not measure what is required on the job. Title VII, for example, requires that such a connection be established. Two deans of a law school in Antioch, California, have stated that minority students who do poorly on written tests do quite well in practical situations. And in a study conducted by the Temple University Medical School, it was found that minorities scoring below the median on an objective test in pathology were performing above the average on a clinical test in pathology designed by the same instructors (Hoover, 1987).

TO TEST OR NOT TO TEST

Those of us who are accountable to our communities must insist on tests. The Nairobi Day School's favorite statement on testing was that "when we get through with a fellow, he can take my test, your test, or anybody's test" (Wilks, 1990) — once taught. The rationale for testing was as follows:

> Student test scores in the local District, which were published in the local papers twice a year, demonstrated the utter failure of the public school in educating the children in the community. Though Nairobi personnel were strongly opposed to excessive reliance on testing and were aware of the deleterious effects of tests on children of color, they were determined to prove that Black children could learn in a Black environment. Balanced, sensitive use of standardized tests was the only way to prove this. (Hoover, 1992)

THE SEARCH FOR A CULTURALLY FAIR TEST

Locating appropriate teaching materials for Ebonics speakers and other miseducated students has been stated to be the goal of many urban school districts, yet there appears to be no such interest in appropriate assessment instruments to measure the achievement. For example, many have accepted the thirty years of research by Chall, Foorman, and others, revealing that African-American and other bilingual/bidialectal children perform better when taught a "balanced" approach to reading with both phonics and literature utilized. Yet, oddly enough, there is no concomitant interest in finding the least biased test to measure the reading achievement. Incredibly, on occasion, the lack of interest approximates purposeful misassessment: *The Technical Manual for the Florida Teacher Certification Examination* (cited in Hoover, 1984) states: "A high rate of failure, particularly for Black students ... possibly will result" from the test.

We must force our districts to not only adopt proven approaches to reading, but also to adopt a fair test. What are the elements of such a test?

Vocabulary, which has been estimated to constitute a large component of comprehension, again actually provides an unbiased assessment of reading comprehension. Though vocabulary items can be reflective of certain classes and geographical areas, they are less subject to the ambiguity, lack of validity, and trickery that is often characteristic of multiple-choice comprehension items.

Another relatively unbiased assessment, the Nairobi Method, now called the One-Two-Three Method (Hoover, Daniels, Lewis, et al., 1989) is the use of simple recall multiple-choice questions following the oral reading of a short paragraph containing most of the spelling patterns of English as a decoding assessment. Comprehension is tested by a series of questions based on simple recall rather than the culture-bound inference formats. The students then write a short composition using information from the orally read paragraph.

Ebonics-speaking students should be tested not only in Standard English but also in Ebonics. A battery of tests developed at Stanford University (Hoover, et al., 1996) and administered to several hundred students, measured students' proficiency in Ebonics and in Standard English in three dimensions: discrimination, repetition, and production. Interestingly enough, those students who were bidialectal, that is, proficient in both language varieties, also tested higher on standardized reading tests.

School administrators who purchase the tests must consult fair test advocates. If administrators rejected biased tests and aggressively insisted on the development of a fair test, we would not have the biased state of affairs that we have. For example, an official in Atlanta Mayor Andrew Young's office called in a host of experts, including the author of this article, to evaluate an entrance exam that was given to prospective city police officers. The evaluators found that the test was extremely biased against minority officers and recommended a multitude of changes before the test could be considered fair. The changes would have been so expensive that the test writer withdrew his contract. New tests were written but were unfortunately eliminated with the ouster of the official who brought in the test bias consultants (Wiley, 1990).

In conclusion:

> We have a mistaken notion that we should concentrate on testing school children rather than on teaching them; on blaming and embarrassing school children for low test scores instead of teaching and nourishing them; on decapitating ... teachers professionally by holding them up to public ridicule and scorn ... because of their test scores rather than encouraging them and teaching them how to teach children. (Hilliard, 1992, p. 35)

And Weinstein (1997) tells us, in his excellent debunking of *The Bell Curve*'s statistical bias and its rejection of any educational solutions for poor children: "Instead of its sighing surrender to supposed genetic destiny for poor children, there's a corrected message: Teach them."

MONIQUE
BRINSON

America the beautiful, who are you
beautiful for?

Jonathan Kozol, Savage Inequalities

The duality of my existence as an African in America is a paradox that is not easily explainable by a hyphen.

I am a twenty-seven-year-old African-American educator and have taught both first and second grade for three years in the Boston public schools. I am fortunate to have found a school that is aligned with my politics and commitments: the Young Achievers Science and Math Pilot School (YASM), an elementary school in the Mission Hill section of Roxbury. I am invested in Roxbury; it was where I was reared and currently make my home. I eat, think, breath, and work in the community. The language of the community is my language.

For my students who speak Ebonics fluently, I want to help them use their language to communicate in Standard English. I try to convey that speaking Standard English does not diminish one's Blackness or "bein down," nor is it "talkin white." Rather, I try to demystify Standard English and explain that it is how mainstream America communicates.

EDUCATIONAL COSTS

I am a product of a desegregation program that provides urban children of color the "opportunity" to attend school in suburban communities. For me, a "quality education" came at the expense of the painful silencing of my identity as an African-American woman. It was in private and suburban systems where the process of acculturation turned quickly into appropriation and then almost complete assimilation. I masked my Blackness and took on the demeanor (speech, dress, bodily movements, and gestures) of my affluent white peers. I began to disassociate myself from my African-American peers. By the age of ten, I had learned that because I had "mastered" Standard English, I had access, unlike my other "bused" peers who carried our Black urban idiosyncrasies, nuances, culture and traditions with each word they uttered. I became well versed in how to blur, blend, and dismiss my Blackness the moment my school bus departed from Roxbury for the suburb of Newton.

Over the years, while at the best of America's schools, my passion for school and learning turned to rage, which eventually led to complete indifference toward my education. Ultimately, this is what motivated me to return to my home community to educate the children (Delpit, 1995). I did not want any child to suffer, as I had, from feelings of inferiority and self-hate, separation from one's culture, and loss of the love for learning.

INCORPORATION OF EBONICS

I use a variety of pedagogical approaches to help students become fluent readers, writers, and orators: the responsive classroom model; whole language approach; cooperative learning; small and whole-group instruction; peer teaching and peer tutoring; and inter-age and cross-grade collaborations and activities. In this essay, I will describe how I use Ebonics, the home/community language of some of the children at YASM.

One example involves taking a traditional poem or piece of literature written in Standard English and juxtaposing it with Black vernacular. I might, for instance, begin with the poem "Boa Constrictor" by Shel Silverstein, a white male author. The poem is written in a standard colloquial format. After completing a series of skill-based activities, outlined by Janiel Wagstaff in *Analogy Minilessons,* my students and I eventually reinvent the poem using Ebonics (Wagstaff, 1994, pp. 15–30).

Boa Constrictor
(Author's Format)

Oh, I'm being eaten
By a boa constrictor
A boa constrictor,
A boa constrictor
I'm being eaten by a boa constrictor,
And I dont't like it — one bit.
Well, what do you know?
It's nibbling my toe.
Oh, gee,
It's up to my knee,
Oh my,
It's up to my thigh,
Oh, fiddle,
It's up to my middle,
Oh, heck,
It's up to my neck, oh, dread,
It's up mmmmmmmmmmmfffffffff

Boa Constrictor
(Oral rendition of Ebonics format)

Ohh, I'm bein'
eatin
By a boa
constricta,
A boa
constricta,
A boa
constricta,
I'm bein' eatin
By a boa
constricta,

And don't like it
one bit.
Wella, whaddah yo' kno?
It's nibblin'
my toe.
Ohh, geeh,
It's uptah my knee,
Ohh my
It's uptah
my thigh,
Ohh fiddl,
It's uptah
my middl,
Ohh hec
It's uptah my
nec,
Ohh, dread
It's
Upmmmmmmmffffffff

The students and I use rap, metaphors, and bodily kinesthetics to interpret the poem. Not only are the affective, cognitive, and psychomotor domains integrated — so that literature/words/text have an expanded meaning — but the children are able to critically engage and invest in their learning (Jacobsen, Eggen, Kauchak, 1989).

More specifically, these are the steps that the children and I move through:

• I read the poem using a monotone voice.

• The children read the poem chorally, also using a monotone voice.

• Children and I reread the poem using chanting and dramatic performance while retaining the language of the author. (For example, "Well, what do you know? It's nibblin' my toe. . . ." While saying this, students bend over and touch their own toe.)

• Next, we read the poem using the cadences, rhythms, and phonology of Ebonics. (We 'funk it up and bring it home!')

• Finally, from chanting we move on to "rappin'" the poem, using rhyming, cadence, call and response, bodily kinesthetic, dramatic repetition, and gestures while "acting out" highlighted vocabulary in the poem, using contemporary Hip-Hop rhythms, dance, and aesthetics.

An observer, watching my students' culminating performance of this poem, would witness the uncensored behaviors and actions of children at "free play" or during recess, removed from adult supervision. The children use the rhymes, rhythms, and cadences created by African Americans. It is this use of Ebonics that validates many of my students and gets them "turned on," "fired up," and collectively engaged.

To facilitate the learning of Standard English, I then ask the class: "Is nibblin' a real word?" (I select a child or team of students to look up the word in the dictionary and share the results with the class.) We then collectively investigate and compare the spelling and meaning of the word "nibblin'" with the word "nibbling."

After investigation and discussion, I try to make a connection between poetry and larger language issues. I explain to the class how poetry is a use of language/genre through which authors express their point of view, using their own creative and artistic stylization in their writing. I explain that the words "heck," "gee," and "nibblin'" that are in Silverstein's poem are not Standard English words but colloquiums, and that the author's deletion of the final *g* is similar to one of the many features of Black vernacular language. I point out that just as poetry is a creative representation of an artist, Ebonics captures the creativity and the inventiveness of a people.

MODELING STANDARD ENGLISH

When children have difficulty learning Standard English, I teach by modeling the rules of Standard English, both orally and in writing. A child might read a story from his or her writing journal, for instance. The student will say a word that they want to learn how to spell "conventionally." I then model speaking, writing, and reading the word. I also place it on the child's "Word Ring," which is the student's personal dictionary of words they often see and use. The student then returns to his or her desk, copies the word, and draws an illustration that matches the text. By using these techniques consistently and over time, children become proficient writers and orators in Standard English and Ebonics.

Ebonics is effective in teaching literacy because it is spelled the way it is spoken. When asking children to use developmental writing techniques, I might say, "Just sound it out." Because Ebonics is phonetically structured, it frees students to focus on their own ideas and to use their own language and creativity in their journal writing. I also use other literacy activities to help my students acquire the conventions of Standard English. These include grammar instruction, writing workshop, and lessons designed to improve reading comprehension and the ability to critically reflect on literature.

I am honored and privileged to have had the opportunity to work with and learn from the children and families in my school community. This essay does not fully display the genius and power of my students' fluent voices, words, and actions as they communicate with the world in both tongues: Standard English and Ebonics. As my students' and I would eloquently describe ourselves, "We got it goin' on!"

4   The Oakland Resolution

Following is the full text of the "Resolution of the Board of Education Adopting the Report and Recommendations of the African-American Task Force," passed on December 18, 1996.

WHEREAS, numerous validated scholarly studies demonstrate that African-American students as a part of their culture and history as African people possess and utilize a language described in various scholarly approaches as "Ebonics" (literally Black sounds) or "Pan-African Communication Behaviors" or "African Language Systems"; and

WHEREAS, these studies have also demonstrated that African Language Systems are genetically based and not a dialect of English; and

WHEREAS, these studies demonstrate that such West and Niger-Congo African languages have been officially recognized and addressed in the mainstream public educational community as worth of study, understanding, or application of its principles, laws and structures for the benefit of African-American students both in terms of positive appreciation of the language and these students' acquisition and mastery of English language skills; and

WHEREAS, such recognition by scholars has given rise over the past fifteen years to legislation passed by the State of California recognizing the unique language stature of descendants of slaves, with such legislation being prejudicially and unconstitutionally vetoed repeatedly by various California state governors; and

WHEREAS, judicial cases in states other than California have recognized the unique language structure of African-American pupils, and such recognition by courts has resulted in court-mandated educational programs which have substantially benefited African-American children in the interest of vindicating their equal protection of the law rights under the Fourteenth Amendment to the United States Constitution; and

WHEREAS, the Federal Bilingual Education Act (20 U.S.C. 1402 *et seq.*) mandates that local educational agencies "build their capacities to establish, implement and sustain programs of instruction for children and youth of limited English proficiency"; and

WHEREAS, the interests of the Oakland Unified School District in providing equal opportunities for all of its students dictate limited English proficient educational programs recognizing the English language acquisition and improvement skills of African-American students are as fundamental as is application of bilingual education principles for others whose primary languages are other than English; and

WHEREAS, the standardized tests and grade scores of African-American students in reading and language arts skills measuring their application of English skills are substantially below state and national norms and that such deficiencies will be remedied by application of a program featuring African Language Systems principles in instructing African-American children both in their primary language and in English; and

WHEREAS, standardized tests and grade scores will be remedied by application of a program with teachers and aides who are certified in the methodology of featuring African Language Systems principles in instructing African-American children both in their primary language and in English. The certified teachers of these students will be provided incentives including, but not limited to, salary differentials.

NOW, THEREFORE, BE IT RESOLVED that the Board of Education officially recognizes the existence, and the cultural and historic bases of West and Niger-Congo African Language Systems, and each language as the predominantly primary language of African-American students; and

BE IT FURTHER RESOLVED that the Board of Education hereby adopts the report, recommendations and attached Policy Statement of the District's African-American Task Force on language stature of African-American speech; and

BE IT FURTHER RESOLVED that the Superintendent in conjunction with her staff shall immediately devise and implement the best possible academic program for imparting instruction to African-American students in their primary language for the combined purposes of maintaining the legitimacy and richness of such language whether it is known as "Ebonics," "African Language Systems," "Pan-African Communication Behaviors" or other description, and to facilitate their acquisition and mastery of English language skills; and

BE IT FURTHER RESOLVED that the Board of Education hereby commits to earmark District general and special funding as is reasonably necessary and appropriate to enable the Superintendent and her staff to accomplish the foregoing; and

BE IT FURTHER RESOLVED that the Superintendent and her staff shall utilize the input of the entire Oakland educational community as well as state and federal scholarly and educational input in devising such a program; and

BE IT FURTHER RESOLVED that periodic reports on the progress of the creation and implementation of such an educational program shall be made to the Board of Education at least once per month commencing at the Board meeting of December 18, 1996.

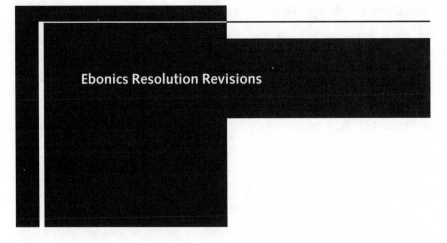

Ebonics Resolution Revisions

A revised edition of the Ebonics resolution was presented to the Oakland school board on January 12 by the Task Force on the Education of African-American Students. Some of the changes, subsequently adopted by the school board, include the following as reported by the Associated Press.

Before: "WHEREAS, these studies have also demonstrated that African Language Systems are genetically based and not a dialect of English."

Changed to: "WHEREAS, these studies have also demonstrated that African Language Systems have origins in West [African] and Niger-Congo languages and are not merely dialects of English."

Before: "WHEREAS, the standardized tests and grade scores . . . will be remedied by application of a program featuring African Language Systems principles in instructing African-American children both in their primary language and in English."

Changed to: "WHEREAS, the standardized tests and grade scores . . . will be remedied by application of a program featuring African Language Systems principles to move students from the language patterns they bring to school to English proficiency."

Before: "The Superintendent . . . shall immediately devise and implement the best possible academic program for imparting instruction to African-American students in their primary language for the combined purposes of maintaining the legitimacy and richness of such language . . . and to facilitate their acquisition and mastery of English language skills."

Changed to: "The Superintendent ... shall immediately devise and implement the best possible academic program for the combined purposes of facilitating the acquisition and mastery of English language skills, while respecting and embracing the legitimacy and the richness of the language patterns."

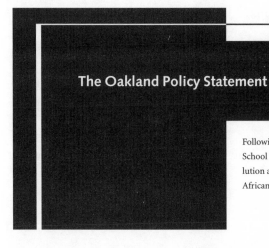

The Oakland Policy Statement

Following is the "Policy Statement of the Oakland School Board" that accompanied the original resolution adopting the recommendations of the African-American Task Force.

There is persuasive empirical evidence that, predicated on analysis of the phonology, morphology and syntax that currently exists as systematic, rule-governed and predictable patterns exist in the grammar of African-American speech. The validated and persuasive linguistic evidence is that African Americans (1) have retained a West and Niger-Congo African linguistic structure in the substratum of their speech and (2) by this criteria are not native speakers of a Black dialect or any other dialect of English.

Moreover, there is persuasive empirical evidence that, owing to their history as United States slave descendants of West and Niger-Congo origin, to the extent that African Americans have been born into, reared in, and continue to live in linguistic environments that are different from the Euro-American English- speaking population, African-American people and their children are from home environments in which a language other than English language is dominant within the meaning of "environment where a language other than English is dominant" as defined in Public Law 1-13-382 (20 U.S.C. 7402, *et seq.*).

The policy of the Oakland Unified School District (OUSD) is that all pupils are equal and are to be treated equally. Hence, all pupils who have difficulty speaking, reading, writing or understanding the English language and whose difficulties may deny to them the opportunity to learn successfully in classrooms where the language of instruction is English or to participate fully in our society are to be treated equally regardless of their race or national origin.

As in the case of Asian-American, Latino-American, Native American and all other pupils in this district who come from backgrounds or environments where a language other than English is dominant, African-American pupils shall not, because of their race, be subtly dehumanized, stigmatized, discriminated against or denied.

Asian-American, Latino-American, Native American and all other language different children are provided general funds for bilingual education, English as a Second Language (ESL) and State and Federal (Title VIII) Bilingual Education programs to address their limited and non-English proficient (LEP/NEP) needs. African-American pupils are equally entitled to be tested and, where appropriate, shall be provided general funds and State and Federal (Title VIII) bilingual education and ESL programs to specifically address their LEP/NEP needs.

All classroom teachers and aides who are bilingual in Nigerian Ebonics (African-American Language) and English shall be given the same salary differentials and merit increases that are provided to the teachers of the non-African-American LEP pupils in the OUSD.

With a view toward assuring that parents of African-American pupils are given the knowledge base necessary to make informed decisions, it shall be the policy of the OUSD that all parents of LEP (Limited English Proficient) pupils are to be provided the opportunity to partake of any and all language and culture-specific teacher education and training classes designed to address their child's LEP needs.

On all home language surveys given to parents of pupils requesting home language identification or designations, a description of the District's programmatic consequences of their choices will be contained.

Nothing in the Policy shall preclude or prevent African-American parents who view their child's LEP as being nonstandard English, as opposed to being West and Niger-Congo African Language based, from exercising their right to choose and to have their child's speech disorders and English Language deficits addressed by special education and/or other District programs.

When I need to say words that do more than simply mirror or address the dominant reality, I speak black vernacular. There, in that location, we make English do what we want it to do. We take the oppressor's language and turn it against itself. We make our words a counterhegemonic speech, liberating ourselves in language.

bell hooks
Teaching to Transgress

There was a mood in the audience of taking a stand, reclaiming a piece of territory. This territory is the classroom. What we want is for African-American people to feel ownership of the classroom. Not to feel shut out. This is what this is about.

Anthony Cody
an Oakland middle school teacher describing the Oakland school board public hearing on January 8, 1997, on the Ebonics resolution

Recommendations of the Task Force on Educating African-American Students

Following are the recommendations of the Task Force on Educating African-American Students regarding cultural-linguistic literacy. The recommendations specify the outcome desired, and the recommended conditions to help meet that outcome. They were adopted on January 21, 1997.

Outcome: OUSD [Oakland Unified School District] shall recognize that most African-American children speak a language other than English in the home.

Recommended Conditions to Be Met: The OUSD Board shall adopt a policy that recognizes that African-American children speak a language other than English in the home.

Outcome: All African-American students shall become proficient in reading, speaking, and writing standard English.

Recommended Conditions to Be Met: (a) OUSD shall administer a language assessment test that measures English proficiency with a uniform instrument throughout the district. (b) School site staff shall maintain a cadre of teachers who are qualified to administer the assessment instrument.

Outcome: African-American pupils who are assessed as limited English proficient shall be identified in all relevant district documents LEP.

Recommended Conditions to Be Met: African-American students identified as LEP in all relevant district documents and included in all grant applications as LEP shall receive all LEP entitlements.

Outcome: Language arts materials that teach reading shall represent proven approaches to teaching bilingual students.

Recommended Conditions to Be Met: (a) OUSD shall adopt language arts materials for all students that represent a phonic-linguistic approach to reading which is inclusive of culturally diverse and historically accurate fiction and nonfiction literature written by and about African Americans.

(b) School sites shall purchase an adequate number of materials to address the cultural-linguistic literacy needs of African-American students, especially those below the levels of benchmark performance standards.

(c) OUSD shall provide library and media resources to include the literature and contributions which reflect the culture of African-American students and include materials developed and/or authored by African-American persons.

(d) OUSD shall train a cadre of parents, family, and community members to review, evaluate, and monitor phonic-linguistic instructional materials as well as other literary genre.

Outcome: Teachers and administrators shall respect and acknowledge the history, culture, and language the African-American student brings to school.

Recommended Conditions to Be Met: (a) OUSD shall provide staff development to teachers, counselors, and administrators that explores attitudes and develops a cultural knowledge base of African Americans.

(b) Staff development shall prepare teachers and administrators to establish an environment that is conducive for teaching and learning.

(c) Staff shall utilize effective instructional pedagogy that addresses the cultural-linguistic differences of African-American students.

(d) Staff shall evaluate the effectiveness of instructional materials as measured by student achievement in all curriculum areas.

Outcome: African-American students shall receive core instruction in Standard English.

Recommended Conditions to Be Met: OUSD shall provide training to staff in teaching the African-American LEP student.

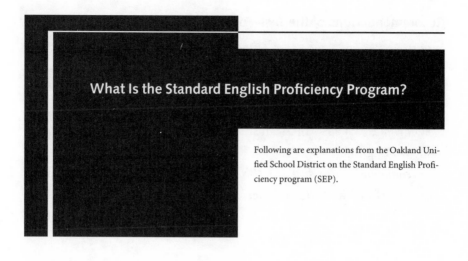

What Is the Standard English Proficiency Program?

Following are explanations from the Oakland Unified School District on the Standard English Proficiency program (SEP).

WHAT IS SEP?

The Standard English Proficiency program (SEP) is a cultural-linguistic program which empowers African-American students with knowledge and understanding of African and African-American culture and languages. Classroom instruction demonstrates the differences in the language spoken in the student's home and Standard English. The teacher and school community embrace the language the students bring to the classroom and build a bridge to Standard English. The teacher and school community acknowledge and understand the student's language. Students may cross the bridge from the language they speak to Standard English with pride and dignity. The student understands and accepts the need to be able to communiate effectively in Standard English in appropriate situations. The framework of the curriculum includes a variety of teaching methods and literary genre to prepare students for the global economy of the twenty-first century.

ENGLISH LANGUAGE DEVELOPMENT GUIDING PRINCIPLES FOR EDUCATORS

- A child's language represents the norm of his or her family and community.

- If a child can express a concept in any language, he or she possesses the concept.
- The teacher must provide as realistic a contextfor language experiences as possible, using materials from the child's culture.
- The child's self-identity must be supported at all times.
- The history of the social isolation (de facto and de jure) of Africans in diaspora has served to preserve African Language patterns of speech.
- African-American Language is a complete, well-ordered language system with rules for forming sounds, words, sentences, and nonverbal elements.

ENGLISH LANGUAGE DEVELOPMENT BASIC ASSUMPTIONS

- The unique history and culture of each child must be recognized and respected.
- The dignity of a person is not guaranteed unless the dignity of his or her people is preserved.
- Language is an integral part of pne's culture.
- Teaching methodology must accommodate the culture and language of the child.
- Acceptance and appreciation of one's native language and culture enhances second language learning.
- Students are enhanced intellectually and academically by the mastery of many languages.

Oakland Superintendent Responds to Critics of the
Ebonics Policy

CAROLYN
GETRIDGE

This article originally appeared in the *Montclarion*,
December 31, 1996. Reprinted with permission of
the author.

On December 18 the Oakland Unified School District Board of Education
approved a policy affirming Standard American English language development for all students. This policy mandates that effective instructional
strategies be utilized to ensure that every child has the opportunity to
achieve English language proficiency.

Language development for African-American students, who comprise
53 percent of students in the Oakland schools, will be enhanced with the
recognition and understanding of the language structures unique to
many African-American students.

This language has been studied by scholars for decades and is referred
to as "Ebonics" or "Pan-American Communication Behaviors" or "African Language Systems." Research indicates that an understanding of these
language patterns helps students build a bridge to Standard American
English.

The Oakland school board's new policy has touched a nerve across the
country. Talk show lines have been jammed and commentators have
offered virtually nonstop opinion about the policy. Unfortunately, the reaction is based almost entirely on very basic misinterpretations of the
meaning and intent of the policy. In the education that America's public
schools provide to minority children, there are many reasons to despair —
but this policy is not one of them. Let me try to start the process of setting
the record straight.

First, Oakland Unified School District is not replacing the teaching of

Standard American English with any other language. The district is not teaching Ebonics. Nothing could be further from the intent of this policy. Our district emphasizes teaching Standard American English and has set a high standard of excellence for all of its students.

Second, Oakland is providing its teachers and parents with the tools to address the diverse language needs that children bring into the classroom. This is not new. For over a decade our district has instituted the Standard English Proficiency program (SEP), a state of California model program, which promotes English language development for African-American students. The SEP training enables teachers to build on the history, culture, and language that many African-American students bring to school. The new board policy takes these practices to all schools throughout our district.

Third, this policy is not an attempt to reallocate bilingual education funding. We are fully committed to incorporating this training into the professional development of our teachers and, if necessary, redirecting present funds to this end. We have not requested any state or federal funds for this purpose.

ADDRESSING AN URGENT NEED

The directions set forth in this policy hold the promise for the positive, sound changes we must make in our nation's schools, which historically have failed African-American students. The low level of African-American student achievement is a national disgrace. One root cause of this dismal performance is the belief held by many that African-American and other minority children are in some way deficient intellectually, socially, and even in their mastery of language.

Committed to seeking strategies to address this dire situation, the Oakland Board of Education formed a broad-based task force in June 1996. The Task Force on the Education of African-American Students established a process to review district-wide achievement data and make recommendations for proven practices that would enhance the opportunity for all students to access and to successfully achieve the core curriculum. The recommendations of the task force, based on academic research, focus on the direct connection of English language proficiency to student achievement, the unique language needs of many African-American pupils, and the opportunities for parents and the community to support improved academic achievement.

The findings on student achievement in Oakland are evidence that the current system is not working for most African-American children. While 53 percent of the students in the Oakland Unified School District are African American, only 37 percent of the students enrolled in Gifted and Talented classes are African American, and yet 71 percent of the students enrolled in Special Education are African American.

The grade point average of African-American students is 1.80 compared to the district average of 2.40; 64 percent of students who repeat the same grade are African American; 67 percent of students classified as truant are African American; 80 percent of all suspended students are African American; and only 81 percent of the African-American students who make it to the twelfth grade actually graduate.

These statistics are both mind-numbing and a cause for moral outrage. The situation has not improved itself during the decade of reform launched by the landmark report, *A Nation at Risk*, and yet there has been little public reaction to the failure of our public schools to educate minority children. Now, however, in response to a straightforward policy to improve teaching and learning, many in the public have readily misunderstood it and made it the occasion for scorn and derision.

The question is not whether or not we must act; rather we are confronted by questions about how best to act, and how quickly can we act? The answers to these questions are not simple and they are not comforting. Quite to the contrary, the answers to these questions challenge some of the fundamental assumptions we have about the purpose and design of education.

The work of the Task Force on the Education of African-American Students provides us with a means to focus our attention where it is most urgently needed. Our focus on African-American student achievement is all the more compelling because of the fact that if we find ways to help the least successful students, we will benefit all of our students.

The recommendations establish English language proficiency as the foundation for competency in all academic areas. Passage of this policy is a clear demonstration that the Oakland Unified School District is committed to take actions to turn around the educational achievement of its African-American students.

Furthermore, the actions of the Oakland Board of Education have elevated the level of the debate on the education of African-American children.

I welcome this debate and I am confident that, as a result, we will move Oakland and the nation to an open discussion of the connection between language and literacy.

We must confront this issue head on, for our achievements in public education will ultimately be judged by how well the least successful of our children perform.

The following resolution was passed by the Linguistic Society of America at its January 3, 1997, meeting in Chicago.

WHEREAS there has been a great deal of discussion in the media and among the American public about the December 18, 1996, decision of the Oakland school board to recognize the language variety spoken by many African-American students and to take it into account in teaching Standard English, the Linguistic Society of America, as a society of scholars engaged in the scientific study of language, hereby resolves to make it known that:

(a) The variety known as "Ebonics, African-American Vernacular English" (AAVE), and "Vernacular Black English" and by other names is systematic and rule-governed like all natural speech varieties. In fact, all human linguistic systems — spoken, signed, and written — are fundamentally regular. The systematic and expressive nature of the grammar and pronunciation patterns of the African-American vernacular has been established by numerous scientific studies over the past thirty years. Characterizations of Ebonics as "slang," "mutant," "lazy," "defective," "ungrammatical," or "broken English" are incorrect and demeaning.

(b) The distinction between "languages" and "dialects" is usually made more on social and political grounds than on purely linguistic ones. For example, different varieties of Chinese are popularly regarded as *dialects*, though their speakers cannot understand each other, but speakers of Swedish and Norwegian, which are regarded as separate "languages," generally understand each other. What is important from a linguistic and educational point of view is not whether AAVE is called a "language" or a "dialect," but rather that its systematicity be recognized.

(c) As affirmed in the LSA Statement of Language Rights (June 1996), there are individual and group benefits to maintaining vernacular speech varieties and there are scientific and human advantages to linguistic diversity. For those living in the United States there are also benefits in acquiring Standard English, and resources should be made available to all who aspire to mastery of Standard English. The Oakland school board's commitment to helping students master Standard English is commendable.

(d) There is evidence from Sweden, the United States, and other countries that speakers of other varieties can be aided in their learning of the standard variety by pedagogical approaches which recognize the legitimacy of the other varieties of a language. From this perspective, the Oakland school board's decision to recognize the vernacular of African-American students in teaching them Standard English is linguistically and pedagogically sound.

This action is a cry for judicial help in opening the doors to the establishment. Plaintiffs' counsel says that it is an action to keep another generation from becoming functionally illiterate.

The failure of the defendant Board to provide leadership and help for its teachers in learning about the existence of "black English" as a home and community language of many black students and to suggest to those same teachers ways and means of using that knowledge in teaching black children code switching skills in connection with reading standard English is not rational in light of existing knowledge on the subject.

Federal Judge Charles Joiner
July 12, 1979

"What Go Round Come Round": *King* in Perspective

GENEVA SMITHERMAN

That teacher, he too mean. He be hollin at us and stuff.

Browny, he real little, he six, and he smart cause he know how to read . . .

Two of the plaintiff children
in the "Black English" case,
King v. Ann Arbor

This essay is adapted and condensed from an article that appeared in the *Harvard Educational Review*.

When the Oakland school board passed its Ebonics resolution in December 1996, its action was a continuation of a struggle over language and education that goes back decades. One of the key battles in that struggle is what is known as the "Black English case" — a 1979 federal court decision affirming the legitimacy of Black English and mandating appropriate measures to teach Standard English to those children speaking Black English.

The case, *Martin Luther King Junior Elementary School Children v. Ann Arbor School District Board*, was as much about educating Black children as about Black English. As Judge Charles W. Joiner, who issued the decision in the case, said: "It is a straightforward effort to require the court to intervene on the children's behalf to require the defendant School District Board to take appropriate action to teach them to read in the standard English of the school, the commercial world, the arts, science, and professions. This action is a cry for judicial help in opening the doors to the establishment. . . . It is an action to keep another generation from becoming functionally illiterate."

The *King* case, filed in 1977 and decided in 1979, was the first test of the applicability to Black English speakers of the language provision of the 1974 Equal Educational Opportunity Act (EEOC). As the plaintiff children's chief consultant and expert witness during the two years of litigation, I shall provide an analysis of *King* and some of its implications.

The background facts of the case are as follows. On July 28, 1977, Attorneys Gabe Kaimowitz and Kenneth Lewis of Michigan Legal Services filed suit in federal Eastern District Court in Detroit on behalf of fifteen Black, economically deprived children residing in a low-income housing project in Ann Arbor. By the time the case came to trial in the summer of 1979, one family with four children had moved out of the school district, leaving eleven plaintiff children.

Initially, the case was directed against the State of Michigan, the Ann Arbor School District, and officials at Martin Luther King Junior Elementary School, where black children comprised 13 percent of the school population of predominantly white, upper-class children. The allegation was that the defendants had failed to properly educate the children, who were thus in danger of becoming functionally illiterate. Specifically, the plaintiffs charged that school officials had improperly placed the children in learning disability and speech pathology classes; that they had suspended, disciplined, and repeatedly retained the children at grade level without taking into account their social, economic, and cultural differences; and that they had failed to overcome language barriers preventing the children from learning Standard English and learning to read. Actions taken by school officials, such as labeling the children "handicapped" and providing them with museum trips and other types of "cultural exposure," had failed to solve the academic problems of the children.

The attitude of school officials was that the school had done its job, and that perhaps the children were uneducable. Yet close scrutiny of the academic records and psychological and speech and language evaluations failed to uncover any inherent limitations in the children's cognitive or language capacities. Further, the children's mothers were not persuaded that the academic and behavioral problems were due to slowness or mental retardation. The mothers' intuition was corroborated by professional judgment: their children were normal intelligent kids who could learn if properly taught.

During the pretrial stage of *King*, Judge Joiner tried to settle the case out of court. The "friends of King," as we, the children's advocates, came to call ourselves, prepared a reading program which the school officials rejected. The complaint was revised and amended several times to comply with Joiner's orders. The most critical revision was that all claims relative to economic, social, and cultural factors were dismissed on constitutional grounds. To put it bluntly, Judge Joiner stressed that the U.S. Constitution can provide protection on the basis of being Black but not on the basis of being poor.

NARROWED TO LANGUAGE CONCERNS

In Judge Joiner's reasoning, it was necessary to focus the issues in *King* solely on section 1703(f) of the EEOC, which reads in part: "No state shall deny equal educational opportunity to an individual on account of his or her race, color, sex, or national origin, by . . . the failure to overcome language barriers that impede equal participation by its students in its instructional programs." What began as much more than a "Black English case" would now focus narrowly on language barriers.

Once Judge Joiner ruled this a language case, the Ann Arbor School District immediately filed a motion to dismiss on the grounds that 1703(f) did not apply to Black English speakers but only to those with foreign language backgrounds. Judge Joiner denied Ann Arbor's motion and issued the following ruling that represented our first victory in the case:

> The statutory language places no limitations on the character or source of the language barrier except that it must be serious enough to impede equal participation by . . . students in . . . instructional programs. Barring any more legislative guidance to the contrary, 1703(f) applies to language barriers of appropriate severity encountered by students who speak "Black English" as well as to language barriers encountered by students who speak German.

With the *King* case clearly, if narrowly, focused on language, Joiner outlined four areas to be covered in the plaintiffs' final amended complaints. These areas, which were at the heart of the four-week trial, were:

• Identify the language barriers confronting the plaintiff children;

• Specify how these barriers had impeded the equal participation of the children in the instructional program of King School;

• Set forth the appropriate action that defendants had allegedly failed to take;

• Identify the connections between the defendants' failure to take appropriate action and the race of the plaintiff children.

THE PLAINTIFF'S CASE

The several versions of the complaint had consistently highlighted that the language barriers facing the plaintiff children at King School were based on both structural and nonstructural "interference phenomena." Structural interferences derive from the structural differences between Black English and Standard English — in other words, differing linguistic structures on the levels of phonology, lexico-semantics and/or morpho-syntax. Nonstructural interferences refer to differing attitudes and conflicting values about the two speech systems and the individuals who use them. The structural and nonstructural interference phenomena are actually inextricable, although they are often expressed as a dichotomy in order to create an analytically convenient, if artificial, schema that readily lends itself to empiricism.

However, because the language-dialect conflict remains unresolved among linguists (that is, is Black English a language or a dialect?), language scholars have no consensus on whether there are both structural and nonstructural interferences between speakers of Black English and speakers of Standard English. Although the evidence is not definitive, the best available data and expert judgment, particularly from Black psychologists, seems to suggest that Black English speakers have language-based problems and only those who master code-switching (moving from Black

English to Standard English and back again) make it through the educational system successfully. Because of the inconclusive research data and because of the inadequacy of existing language models to account for differences in discourse structure, the plaintiffs in *King* were unsuccessful in persuading the court that structural linguistic barriers existed. Although Judge Joiner conceded that "there was initially a type of language difference," he reasoned that "it did not pose a communications obstruction" in student-teacher interaction.

Research on socioloinguistics in the educational process has been most fruitful and convincing in uncovering underlying attitudes about language. Therefore, specifying the nature of nonstructural barriers proved to be our most powerful legal strategy.

In the educational context, negative linguistic attitudes are reflected in the institutional policies and practices that become educationally dysfunctional for Black English-speaking children. Research on language attitudes consistently indicates that teachers believe Black English-speaking youngsters are nonverbal and possess limited vocabularies. They are perceived to be slow learners or uneducable. Their speech is seen as unsystematic and is constantly corrected. Thus, they are made somehow to feel inferior.

Since Black English is viewed so pejoratively by Standard English-speaking teachers, it was not difficult to reconstruct the process whereby this language barrier impeded the educational success of the plaintiff children. It was not the Black Language in and of itself that constituted the barrier, but negative institutional policies and classroom practices relative to Black English that were, and are, key causes of Black children's reading problems. Since reading is crucial to academic achievements in all school subjects, the inability to read at grade level prevents equal participation in the educational programs of the school.

What, then, was the appropriate action the school board had failed to take? It had not instituted policies to assist King School teachers and personnel to handle the linguistic and educational needs of the plaintiff children. As Joiner indicated: "The court cannot find that the defendant

School Board had taken steps (1) to help the teachers understand the problem; (2) to help provide them with knowledge about the children's use of a "Black English" language system; and (3) to suggest ways and means of using that knowledge in teaching the students to read."

The relationship between the district's lack of appropriate action and race lies in the manner in which Black English has developed and is maintained as a unique speech system. The speech patterns of Black Americans developed from an African linguistic and cultural base, which was transformed by their experience in the United States. It was reinforced and sustained by racial oppression and segregation, on the one hand, and by the response to racism, in the form of ethnic solidarity, on the other. The institutionalization of racism in America has meant exclusion of Blacks from participation in the dominant culture, and has resulted in the continuance of two separate societies and two distinct, if not entirely separate, languages.

Blacks, however, have been differentially affected by white racism, and that has created class distinctions within the Black community. Differing degrees of competence in Standard English is one way these distinctions are manifest. Not all Black children suffer from language barriers. Indeed, at King, the only Black children having great difficulty were those from the Green Road Housing Project, who were both Black and poor. The other Black children attending King were from middle-class, professional families, and were also competent in Standard English; they were skilled at code-switching and, hence, "bilingual." The economically deprived plaintiff children, not being adequate code-switchers, experienced language-based problems in school. Thus the language barriers for the Green Road children were directly related to both racial and economic discrimination, but Joiner had ruled out economic factors as a matter for consideration.

Put more succinctly, negative language attitudes are directed toward the "Blackness" of Black English; the attitudes and the language itself are the consequences of the historical operations of racism in the United States. To the extent that the district failed to take appropriate action, such failure was connected to the race of the plaintiff children by virtue of their speaking Black English, and the barriers created were therefore directly related to race. This, in turn, obligated the district to take appropriate action under the 1974 EEOC to eliminate the discrimination.

During the actual four-week trial, a biracial team of expert witnesses in the fields of psychology, education, linguistics, and reading testified on behalf of the plaintiff children. The defendant school board called no expert witnesses, but simply relied on cross-examination of the plaintiffs' experts. During the trial, it was established that the school district had failed to recognize the existence and legitimacy of the children's language, Black English. This failure and the corresponding negative attitudes toward the children's language led to negative expectations toward the children which turned into self-fulfilling prophecies. One critical consequence was that the children were not being taught to read.

On July 12, 1979, Judge Joiner issued what he later described as a "rather conservative" ruling: on the basis of failing to overcome language barriers, the Ann Arbor school district had violated the children's right to equal educational opportunity. Though Black English was not found to be a barrier per se, the institutional response to it was a barrier. In short, this ruling affirmed the obligation of school districts to educate Black children and served to establish, within a legal framework, what has been well-documented in academic scholarship: Black English is a systematic, rule-governed language system developed by Black Americans as they struggled to combine the cultures of Africa and the United States.

The educational plan approved by Joiner to remedy the discrimination faced by the Black English speakers at King unfortunately fell far short of the mark. As attorney Kenneth Lewis noted in 1980, the plan "amounts to no more than yet another shot in the arm of teacher inservice programs." Clearly, such programs are desirable and needed to alter teacher attitudes toward Black English. But inservice training should be merely one component of a more comprehensive educational remediation plan that has as its central theme the teaching of reading and other communication skills.

LESSONS LEARNED

Despite the shortcomings of the *King* case, it was an important precedent. Although this is neither the time nor place to outline a comprehensive approach to teaching Standard English to children who speak Black English, there are several important lessons of the *King* case. These include:

• Judicial processes are critical in shaping educational policy and practice. Despite the lament that the courts are too involved in the management of social institutions, the judiciary can promote the just and humane administration of large social bureaucracies that seem incapable of righting themselves.

• We need a school effectiveness policy monitored and enforced by the courts and by appropriate citizens' bodies. Accountability must be demanded and delivered.

• There should be a national moratorium on "tests" — standardized, employment, and other such assessment instruments. All evidence points to the cultural and linguistic biases of such tests.

• Legal legitimacy has been given to a speech form spoken at times by 80–90 percent of the Black community in the United States.

• The viability and appropriateness of Black English should in no way be construed to mean that students should not be taught competence in Standard English.

• The media is not an ally. There were over 300 newspaper and magazine articles and editorials on the case. Yet media sensationalism prevented the issues from being clearly and fully delineated. There was a persistent attempt to discredit the plaintiffs' mothers and to exonerate the school district.

• In some circles, it became fashionable to disavow the need for and utility of academic research. *King*, however reaffirms the need for more, not less, research that is responsive to the needs of Black and other dispossessed communities.

CONCLUSION

There were no spoils to the victors in *King*. Although the ruling set a legal precedent establishing that Black English falls within the parameters of the statutory language of the EEOC, it is an acknowledged reformist strategy. But it is a tool now available to other communities for manipulating the legal system to obtain a measure of redress from our continuing oppression.

The fate of Black children as victims of miseducation continues to be the bottom line in the "Black English case." *King* gives us yet another weapon in our struggle to save the children. The case began with a claim of institutional mismanagement of education for children from the Green Road Housing Project. It ended with a claim of institutional mismanagement of the children's language. For those who know that language is identity, the issue is the same: the children's language is them is they mommas and kinfolk and community and Black culture and the Black experience made manifest in verbal form.

Opening Pandora's Box: An Interview with Oakland School Board Member Toni Cook

Toni Cook has served on the Oakland school board since 1990. It was Cook who prodded her fellow trustees on the board to unanimously support the nation's first education policy recognizing Ebonics as the "primary language" of many students, comparing their language needs with those of immigrant children.

In this interview Cook tells how she came to be at the center of a national debate about language, race, and the education of African-American children.

Cook was interviewed by Nanette Asimov of the *San Francisco Chronicle*. The interview originally appeared January 19, 1997. © 1997 *San Franciso Chronicle*, reprinted with permission.

Other than making a lot of people mad, what have you done here?

I've sounded a bell that everyone is talking about. We got a call from Amsterdam and another one from South Africa. I'm finding that more people are becoming anywhere from supportive to understanding about this.

Has anyone given you serious trouble?

Someone called from a radio talk show and played real raw, racist stuff live and on air. My reaction to the first flood of phone calls (on my answering machine) was to deep-six every call.

Why?

I was broadsided by the controversy. I didn't get home (from the board meeting) until 2 A.M., and I didn't listen to any news the next day because I didn't think anything we did was newsworthy. I'm just thinking, "I can't function." So I get up and make the call (to my job at the San Francisco

Housing Authority): "I'm not coming." Then Edgar, our board's assistant, calls and says, "Can you come over?" I said, "Edgar, I'm trying to put a lie together about why I'm not going to work." He said, "All hell has broken loose on the resolution." I said, "What resolution?" He said, "The one put out by the African-American task force. The mayor's on a rampage."

Why was (Mayor) Elihu Harris so mad?

I used to work for Elihu. He could be mad at anything! And when I got there, he had already gone off to (Superintendent) Carolyn Getridge. And he asked me, "Do you know what you have done? I'm getting calls from everybody in the world! This is embarrassing to Oakland! You all have adopted a policy that's going to teach Black English!"

I said, "Elihu, I know you're cheap, but do you have television? Did you watch the school board meeting last night? We meant you no ill will in terms of your challenges with this city. But our kids are being ridiculed if they speak Standard English — "Ugh, you talk like a white girl!" So this is the problem we're faced with, and this is how we're going to deal with it." Elihu kind of calmed down a little, and we began to focus on why we did it like we did.

What did you do and why did you do it?

I asked the superintendent to form a task force to look at the performance of African-American kids. Since I've been on the board, dropout rates, suspensions, expulsions, truancy — all have gone up for African-American kids. But enrollment in the gifted and talented program and presence in college-bound, honors, and advanced-placement classes were not proportionate to Black enrollment, which is 53 percent.

What about special education?

Of 5,000 kids in that, 71 percent are African American. And they were in there for "causing disruption."

Aren't special education classes supposed to be for students who are disabled or have learning disabilities?

Yes. And you have to have a referral to be placed in the program. The referrals disproportionately were because of a "language deficiency."

What's that?

When you really dug down, it's that they weren't writing or speaking Standard English. We found there were white and Black teachers making referrals. And white and Black principals — disproportionately Black — saying yes. So when the task force began to talk with teachers, it was like, "well, we don't have any strategies for these kids." The only one they had was the (state's) Standard English Proficiency program (SEP) for a few teachers who got the training.

So what did you do?

You know, there's an old guy who comes to the board meetings named Oscar Wright. He came to every board meeting until his wife died about a year ago. And he would stand with those trembling hands and talk about the performance of African-American kids — test scores, truancy — and he said, "I see having four Black board members has made no difference in what these kids are doing."

And we hung our heads, because it was true! We had a crisis situation and we kept coming up with old ways. Or ways that were so homogenized they didn't really wake anybody up.

You're saying that test scores will go up as African-American students begin speaking Standard English?

Yes. Which ultimately means — more critically — that they can go from high school to college if that's their choice. You can no longer drop your kid off in kindergarten and expect to pick him up in the twelfth grade with a diploma that means he's ready for college. We should quit making these promises that we're going to do that by adding health programs, and all those other kinds of things. That is not about education. I know they need all that, but there isn't any education strategy here. When it's directed to African-American kids, it's basically the assumption that we have to control them before we can educate them.

You don't feel that way?

No.

How can you teach a kid who's out of control — whether threatening a teacher or just making noise?

Teachers need the teaching and learning tools to know how to communicate with these youngsters to capture their attention. We have some kids with a proven record of suspension in the third grade, and they're going like this (waves wildly) in the math class! I've seen that at some of our schools in the deepest parts of the flatlands.

Are you saying their teachers caught their attention because they spoke Ebonics?

What they knew was how to hear the child, listen to the child, correct the child, and make the child feel good about being corrected. These are teachers who have been through our SEP program.

Give me an example.

Well, I go to classes to read to the kids. Everybody knows Dr. Seuss, so I made the presumption that I could read a page and the child would read a page. I found two things: Either the kids could not read, or they could read, but the words they pronounced were definitely not on that piece of paper.

What were they saying?

-*ing*'s left off of words, consonants left off words, and you begin to think: "Does this kid have dyslexia? Half the word is falling off." And then I went to Prescott Elementary, and I noticed that in (teacher) Carrie Secret's class, where most of the kids are from the housing projects, they could read, and tell you what they had read, had great diction, good reasoning skills. And this was the third grade.

You're saying that the kids in this class had better diction than kids in other classes with the same background?

Yes. And I began to ask Carrie Secret, "What are you doing differently?" She told me about the SEP program. So when a kid did not make the -ing sound, or left off a consonant, or made a word singular when it should be plural, or plural when it should be singular, Carrie would repeat back to the young people until they began to hear the correct word.

How did she do it?

The child says, "I'm going wit my mother." Or, "I'm goin home." She says, "Where?" And the child says, "I'm going to go home."

When you heard children speaking Standard English, you were thrilled. You're sounding like the critics of your own Ebonics resolution.

Standard English is (necessary) to go to a four-year college, to being accepted in an apprenticeship program, to understanding the world of technology, to communicating. We owe it to our kids to give them the best that we've got.

There's great disagreement over Black English as a language, a language "pattern," or just street slang. What is Black English?

All I know is that it's not slang. The linguists call that "lazy English." But our children come to school with this language pattern. Go back to what they call the Negro spiritual: "I'm going to lay my 'ligion down." That was the code song that got you your ticket on the Underground Railroad. It's the way the words were used. So they might have thought we were old dumb slaves, but it served a purpose. It was communication.

Do some parents and children resist speaking Standard English because they really see it as white English?

I don't think they consciously resist. My youngest daughter has had that criticism: "You talk like a white girl." It's another way of saying, "How come you don't sound like us?" It hurts to be accused of that. When I was a girl, it was a goal to speak Standard English, not a ridicule. I have no idea how that changed.

Why don't children automatically know Standard English, since they hear it all the time on television and at school?

Two things. African Americans whose economic status and exposure is closer to that of the Huxtables have the exposure to work with the youngsters and teach them about the "two-ness" of the world they're involved in. But some schools are located in very depressed areas, have a primary population of African Americans on a fixed income. They see very little, the young people are exposed to very little, and there isn't a whole lot of reason in the home — this is just my guess — to adopt the behavior of duality.

Do you believe that the language pattern of Black English is genetic?

It's ancestral. "Genetic" doesn't say "in your blood, in your biology." It says, "in the beginning!"

Following that logic, why don't other ethnic groups use the grammar of their immigrant ancestors?

No other group in America, outside the Native Americans, ever had to grope (as we did) with the new language. If you didn't get off the Good Ship Lollypop speaking English, learning it was exacerbated by the fact that you had to sneak to teach yourself. Then if you stay together in an isolated, segregated environment, the language pattern persists over time.

And yet there are millions of African Americans who speak with no trace of Ebonics.

And there are an awful lot of second- and third-generation Chinese who speak perfect English, but when they go home to grandmother, they make the switch.

And many African Americans don't. Is this an issue of class?

In some instances, it is class. You know, having come from a family of educators, it was a symbol of your ability to speak the King's English. I remember my mother telling me the tragedy is that as those kids became comfortable with the tools of the middle class, one of which was language, they began to turn their backs on their parents. They were embarrassed about their language style.

This is the traditional immigrant experience. What's unusual is for children to cling to the language patterns of their elders.

Here is where it's confusing to some, but to others, I think they have ulterior motives.

What's the ulterior motive?

The English Only campaign. We talked informally among the school board members. Be careful, don't get caught up in the English Only campaign.

And the ulterior motive is the anti-affirmative action movement?

The funding is from the same platform, right-wing America. It used

to be that we'd just simply say it was racism. But now they are so sophisticated that it's about being anti-Black, anti-Jewish, anti-immigrant, anti
anything that's not Christian. Anti-urban, anti-female, I mean they just
kind of took everybody and threw us all over there together. We have no
allies over there. None whatsoever.

*If nothing else, you've gotten them to add anti-Ebonics to the list. But
you've also gotten many people on your side, haven't you?*

I'd love to be able to tell you how we plotted and planned to become
the topic of everybody's conversation in the world. That's dishonest. It
took me by surprise.

*You had been very opposed to changing any of the controversial wording
in your resolution — that Ebonics is "genetically based," for instance, and
that students will be taught "in Ebonics." Yet you changed your mind.
What happened?*

Sometimes you have to look: Are you winning the battle but losing the
war? The African-American Task Force met (for about ten hours) last
week and got no closure on the word "genetics." Oscar Wright, the old
man of the group, said, "If removal of this word will heal the pain of the
African-American community, then remove the word." When that old
man gave the word, we moved on. I felt fine about that. I would have
stayed on course, but the village said to do things differently.

Did you grow up speaking Ebonics?

No, but I heard it. You've got to think about coming up in a segregated
time. In 1954, when the school desegregation decision came, I was ten. But
the more I think about it, the more I think about how blessed I've been.
Both of my parents had graduate degrees. My dad was a dentist. My mom
was a linguist with the National Security Agency. We were never quite sure
what she really did. We know she spoke perfect Russian. We used to say
Mom was a spy for the FBI. And we always thought that Mommy was the
smartest thing we ever saw.

So language and politics were always entwined in your family?

Everyone in my family, whether it was Mom or Dad, they were always
crusaders. You never earned the right to snub your nose at anybody based

on speech patterns. I remember a time when we went down the street, and a drunk said something to my sister Twink, and she laughed. Mom gave her a backhand, and said, "That man meant nothing but to be kind. Go back and say: "How do you do, sir?" She was serious. My mother was 4-foot-9, and 89 pounds, boy. And she spoke perfect English.

They (the school board) said it's all right to talk the way you talk — that you're not stupid, just different.

Marcus Harrison, an unemployed welder

It's a Black thing, the way Black people talk, and white folks don't like people to act different.

Bernard Simpkins, a truck driver

Proposition 187, Proposition 209, now this. It's easy to see a pattern. They don't want immigrants here, and they don't want us to get jobs. But they want us all to talk the same.

Yolanda Hernandez, teacher's aide
All quoted in the San Francisco Chronicle, *December 23, 1996*

An Oakland Student Speaks Out

MICHAEL LAMPKINS

Following is the testimony by Michael Lampkins, the student director on the Oakland Board of Education. The testimony was given on January 23 at a hearing on Ebonics before the Subcommittee on Labor, Health and Human Services and Education of the Senate Appropriations Committee.

I am a seventeen-year-old high school senior. My grades put me at the top of my class. I work part-time and volunteer my time to help kids. I care for my elderly grandmother. I was elected Youth of the Year by the Boys and Girls Clubs of America. And I have held audience with President Clinton. But when I walk out that door, nine times out of ten, I'm perceived quite differently. I need a solid education. I want to learn. I want teachers and administrators who want me to succeed in my future. I want African-American student counterparts in my classrooms who want to learn. Therefore, I need instructors with the classroom strategies that are right to meet my unique needs growing up in a contemporary urban community.

Just as a doctor must be trained to diagnose the symptoms of disease, teachers must be trained to recognize the language patterns that students bring into the classroom. And, while those language patterns are different than Standard English, they are not deficient, and with the proper instructional methods a bridge is built to transition students to learn to speak, read, and write Standard English proficiently.

As America embarks on the twenty-first century, I come before you with a plea: I want to be part of the "new promise." I want to be prepared with a competitive education and advanced degrees, so that I may take my rightful place as a leader in tomorrow's global workforce.

Ebonics and the Role of the Community: An Interview with Activist Isaac Taggert

Following is an interview with Isaac Taggert, co-founder and co-chair of the Oakland community group Africans United for Self Help. Taggert was a member of the Task Force on Educating African-American students that, as part of a broader program of school reform for the Oakland public schools, recommended what became known as the Ebonics resolution. Taggert was interviewed by Barbara Miner, managing editor of *Rethinking Schools*.

Can you tell us a little about your background?

I grew up in San Francisco in the housing projects. Four years ago I started Do 4 Self Enterprises, an African cultural bookstore. I can't stress enough the importance of our children getting their culture at an early age. We are losing too many of our male students. Without our history, without our culture, you are just out there on your own. You are either caught up in the white bind or selling drugs or becoming an alcoholic. But African culture is what gives people self-esteem and the other motivation that you need to achieve in life. That is why I own a bookstore.

As a community person, how did you become involved with the Oakland public schools?

Two years ago there was a teachers' strike in the public school system. That is when a lot of community people became aware of the need to get involved if we wanted a better education for our children. And after attending the Million Man March in the fall of 1995, African men and women in Oakland organized a group called Africans United for Self Help. The first issue we became involved in was around major redevelopment in Oakland, with hundreds of millions of dollars of construction, including a new football and basketball arena. We basically went out with picket signs demanding not only work but business opportunities for African contractors. And then during the school strike, we focused on the schools. This was long before the Ebonics issue came up. We were fortunate that during the strike, we met with a core group of African teachers who did not strike and who were working countless hours developing curriculums and teaching strategies in a program called the Standard English Proficiency — teachers such as Carrie Secret, Nabeehah Shakir, and Hafeezah Dalji, just to name a few. We were also blessed to have met Dr. Ernie Smith, a linguist who spent countless hours educating us on Ebonics, and Dr. Mary Hoover, who has developed a "superliteracy" curriculum that can teach any child to read.

We started doing further investigation on education. There was the Black English case in Michigan in 1979 (see Geneva Smitherman, page 29), and we found out that in 1981, the state superintendent in California and the state Department of Education had passed a resolution for all school districts to deal with Black Language and the linguistic differences of our children. But nothing was ever done. There was no categorical funding or general funding to assist our children. Instead, what was happening was that they were dumped into the special education classes. Or they were dumped into other language classes, such as English as a Second Language (ESL) classes for Cantonese, Vietnamese, or Spanish speakers, used as fillers* and language models.

I have a son who is seven and in second grade. I also take care of my brother's two children; one is seven and one is nine. So I have three children in the Oakland system. So I am also very personally concerned as a parent. And as for my children, there is no television allowed Monday through Thursday. So for at least three hours they are studying, and playing with one another, and doing some activity other than watching television. They are in bed by 7:30 and up at 6 A.M., ready to go.

What were some of the things that Africans United for Self Help did around education?

---

* If a certain number of children were required for the constitution of an ESL class for Cambodian, Vietnamese, or Spanish-speaking children, African-American children were inappropriately place in these classes and used to fill the remaining slots.

Wearing black outfits, we started going to the school board meetings every two weeks. During the teachers' strike, the white teachers would go and harass the executive board members and the superintendent, the majority of which at the time were Black. The majority of teachers in Oakland are white even though most of the students are Black. We were very concerned because our students were not learning. The white teaching population wanted more money but no accountability and no results.

After speaking with students and those teachers, some of our Black teachers, and principals who really cared, we armed ourselves with the teachers' contract, the principals' contract, laws on education, and existing policies — with the knowledge needed to go in and intelligently address the issues and needs of our babies. For over two years, we have gone every two weeks to the board meetings, relentlessly and persistently pressuring the district's governing board, demanding better opportunities and parity when it came to resources for our children. We have also organized parents at individual schools, and monitored specific schools on a weekly basis. We also picketed some schools. We held a press conference and gave the district a list of demands. We also went to curriculum and instruction meetings. We put on a free education conference to educate parents, teachers, and community people about the Standard English Proficiency program and Ebonics.

We asked for an African-centered curriculum and more African teachers — I use African in order to be inclusive of all African people. We demanded more teachers that reflect the student body. So if 83 percent of the student body is African, we wanted the teaching body to reflect that. Cultural experiences are relevant, and we feel that the teaching staff needs to have the same cultural backgrounds as the students. We turned out educated children during segregation.

Toni Cook, one of the school board members, called for a task force on the education of African-American children. We were putting the pressure on. I became a member of the task force, which operated under the supervision of then Superintendent Carolyn Getridge. The task force was made up of community people, administrators, educators, teachers, clergy, and so forth. Basically, we were to put together a catalog of recommendations of what we felt was needed to educate our children — and I'm not just talking about the talented tenth of the community but the other talented 90 percent. The catalog of recommendations that the task force came up with was over seventeen pages of detailed information that would turn the academic failure of our children around to academic success. Only one of the recommendations dealt with Ebonics, but Ebonics was what the media picked up on.

What the Ebonics recommendation was really about was recognizing and respecting the language that our children bring to the classroom environment and giving teachers the proper strategies and techniques to respectfully take our children from where they are to where they need to go as far as mastering Standard English. The goal for all of us is for our children to have equal protection under the law, and to have nurturing teachers for our children and resources to help them master Standard English.

How would you summarize the role of the community in the education reforms in Oakland?

If the community had not been active, we would have never gotten to this point. We had a majority Black board, we had a Black superintendent, we had a majority Black principals, and they did not deal with the issue of assisting our babies in their linguistic needs. The Negro educators felt they knew what was best for all of our community. The average grade point average was 1.8 for African students; they basically kept that type of information away from the community. For example, we heard of Ebonics last year, but after further investigation we found out about the state board policy from 1981.

Just before the African members lost the majority on the school board, during their last weeks on the job, they finally did what they had to do. Without the community's intervention, without community proactivism, the majority of the educators would have been either looking out for their own self-interest or scared of their job. You know, like with the police, there is the code of silence. Black administrators were also putting our children in bilingual classes, dumping them in special education classrooms. This is what was going on not just in Oakland, but in every city and every state. The educators have not found the answer to educating our babies. The only ones who have done it consistently are our Black independent schools. Isn't it ironic that at the Million Woman March, on the top of the agenda was Black independent schools?

The role of the community — the role of the parent, the role of the uncle, the role of the brother, the role of the father in particular — is so important. I can't stress it enough. If the community is not watching, if we are not involved, if we are not proactive instead of reacting, if we are not demanding that we be equal partners in our children's education, then we are accomplices in their failures.

5 Personal Essays

Toni Morrison pointed out that making black literature was not just a matter of dropping the "g's" but rather the linguistic embodying of particular values. Some of her prose contains gaps — actual spaces between words — which invite reader participation in much the same way a black preacher's pauses allow his congregation to respond. Increasingly, writers use the call/response patterns so central to the vernacular and have invented what Morrison calls "unorthodox novelistic techniques" such as the chorus to elicit group participation.

Barbara Christian
The Norton Anthology of African American Literature

Official Language, Unofficial Reality: Acquiring Bilingual/ Bicultural Fluency in a Segregated Southern Community

JOYCE HOPE SCOTT

Ocala, Florida, is chiefly known today as horse-breeding territory. Numerous horse farms dot the landscape, fixtures of the influx of wealthy retirees, foreign investors, and other real estate speculators in the last twenty-five years. Taking a longer view, however, there is a rich and powerful African legacy in Ocala, located in the north-central region of the Florida peninsula. The very name Ocala is, quite possibly, from the Bantu family of languages in Africa, according to Winifred Kellersberger Vass in her definitive work, *The Bantu Heritage of the United States.* In the nearby St. Augustine area, meanwhile, recent archeological digs have unearthed Fort Mose, the first African settlement in the United States, established in 1738.

One of the most well-known historical aspects of Florida is the relationship between the Seminole Indians and African slaves who fled from Georgia and South Carolina and escaped into Seminole territory. The "mélange" of these two peoples, along with the Spaniards' liberal attitudes toward slaves (Florida was a Spanish colony until 1819), helped to create numerous maroon slave societies around the state. The escaped African slaves' legacy of resistance in turn attracted freed men and women (such as my maternal great-grandmother and her husband and family) to the state after Emancipation.

The Ocala area boasts a particularly impressive history of African-American communities and families. As African Americans in the area received the news of Emancipation, they bought land, established churches, businesses, and private schools (such as the Fessenden and Howard Academies), and organized women's and men's philanthropic clubs. As late as the 1920s, Blacks owned nearly all of the businesses in Ocala's downtown, including The Metropolitan Negro Bank, a cotton gin (half of whose employees were Black and the other half white), a hotel for Negroes, and the boardinghouse known as St. George Hotel.

Ocala's Black community also shared a belief in community and public service, an attitude that grew out of its strong Christian tradition. From 1868 to 1870, Marion County, where Ocala is located, was served by a Black sheriff. Between 1871 and 1879, seven Black men from the Ocala area served in Florida's House of Representatives in Tallahassee. Dr. Carrie Mitchell Hampton, born in Ocala in 1855, is said to be the first woman medical doctor in Florida. In addition to her medical responsibilities, Dr. Hampton owned and operated a drug store on West Broadway in Ocala, which was used by the town's Black people in the segregated city. Another of these outstanding "early pioneers" was Mrs. Delia J. Brown. The first woman mortician in Florida, she completed her training at the Renouard Training School for Embalmers in Harlem, New York, in 1921 and returned to Ocala and established a business.

OCALA AND MY WORLD

This was the tradition into which I was born, and it is where I learned about myself, my community, and my language. I remember, for example, when Mrs. Brown asked my mother to allow my sisters and me to sing in a radio advertisement for her funeral home. To my knowledge, she was the first Black person "bold" enough to demand equal air time from the Ocala radio station. We weren't allowed to come to the station to sing live; the broadcast was done from the parlor of her funeral home.

One of the main concerns of Ocala's Black community was the education of all Black children, with a particular emphasis on community service. Our teachers, pastors, parents, Sunday school leaders, and others advocated the higher purpose *d'être engagée* — to be engaged. If one was "smart," they said, one was obliged to do something with his or her life.

And, in fact, we could see this taking place all around us. People were not just teachers or doctors or pastors; they were also involved in institution-building and economic development. They owned their own homes, businesses, professional services, land and farms. Their own access to the broader market economy was of paramount importance. Many times I heard my father say, "A man ain't got nothing if he ain't got no land of his own, no matter what else he got."

It was most important to be morally upright, which meant being a member — a committed member — of a church. It was not enough to just attend; one had to be involved. When we children reached the age of fifteen or sixteen, we were expected to take our places as teachers of the younger ones during Sunday school classes. This practice extended the learning activities beyond the academic classrooms at school and fed into the formal process that was synonymous with education. As part of this formal process, for Christmas and Easter programs we had to perform speeches, skits, and other presentations for our parents and other community members. These were the "children's days," and all attention was focused on us. I couldn't "mess up" because I would be "shaming" everybody (on both sides of my family) back to my great-grandparents, whose names are engraved on the cornerstone of the Calvary Baptist Church in the Santos area of Ocala.

"Messing up" did not just refer to missing or forgetting lines. It particularly meant "code-switching" to Black English grammar and/or using Black English enunciations — leaving the *g* off an *-ing* word, for example, or putting stress on part of a word where there was none in Standard English. The Sunday school teacher or one of the church mothers would scold you first; then you could count on an older cousin, sister or brother, or your parents to get you when you returned home. What were you going to school for, they'd say, if you couldn't remember how you were supposed to speak in front of an audience, that is, to use your "public voice"? We were taught specifically that we had a public and a private face, and different languages through which the two distinct personas could be animated. These languages were in a dialogic relationship with each other, and our responsibility was to understand and master this linguistic paradigm rather than to perceive the languages as in conflict with each other.

I learned very early, in the home, that there was a place for both languages in our communal experience. My mother taught me the beauty of both Standard and Black English by reading to me when I was young, first the classic fairy tales, then later Dickens and English and American poets. I especially liked her to read the Sunday funnies aloud; sometimes she would ad lib on the characters' dialogue using the Black vernacular. My mother was, and remains, a true storyteller, with a vast repertoire. I always knew what kind of story she was about to tell by the language she slipped into. European tales, such as "East of the Sun and North of the Wind" or the legends of Thor or Zeus, were read or told in Standard English. Local folktales, lore, and African-American animal tales were told in the Black vernacular.

One of my aunts instructed me further, by her example, in the process of code-switching. I could always tell to whom she was speaking on the telephone by her use of language. She had a "formal" Standard English voice and an "informal" Black English voice. She made the distinctions, first of all, in how she identified herself. If she were speaking to someone from the family or a close friend, she would say, "this Sustah," or "yeah," or "no, I ain't." If she were "speaking proper," as we called it, that meant she was talking to either an older or professional person from the Black community or to a white person. At those times, she was "Mamie Lee" or "Miz Boyd," and the responses were always, "yes," "no, I am not," or "no, it isn't." The verb *to be* was used according to Standard English grammatical rules.

EDUCATION AND SCHOOL

School was where language training was routinized. Education was also a formal affair at our local elementary and senior high schools. Between 1950 and 1962, when my brothers and sisters and I attended Belleview-Santos Elementary and High School, it was an all-Black, segregated public school. Instruction extended beyond mere academics to include dress, behavior, and comportment. The educators, who continuously modeled behavior in addition to mentoring us, were concerned with producing young people who would continue in a tradition of academic excellence, moral uprightness, and social commitment. They made it clear that education was not just an end in itself but that we also had an obligation and responsibility to our parents, our community, and our race.

During special events planned by the faculty, we learned even more about responsibility by actually assuming roles of leadership. One of these events was Student Government Week, when students were in charge of the campus. The principal and each of the teachers selected a student from the high school to substitute for them during this week. This was a true honor, for it reflected the teachers' faith and belief in their students. I remember being chosen in different years to teach junior and senior English classes, history classes, and math classes. The faculty never intruded during the week and we never failed them. The students we taught also never questioned our authority. These roles required "formal" behavior and only Standard English could be used. Perhaps it was due to our ability to move so easily between the languages that we were not challenged by our classmates, friends, and younger sisters and brothers.

English classes were designed to teach Standard English. I remember that we devoted the entire first semester of tenth grade to a review of English grammar, which the teacher felt we had not yet mastered. Our reading assignments included the works of Shakespeare, *Beowulf*, *The Canterbury Tales*, and *A Tale of Two Cities*. We also read American classics, which included African-American greats such as Richard Wright, Langston Hughes, Frederick Douglass, and Paul Laurence Dunbar. While I didn't think it remarkable at the time, I now find it fascinating that one of my most brilliant and articulate English teachers read Paul Laurence Dunbar's dialect poetry with a power and facility that I have not witnessed before or since. She could also bring an audience to its feet with her rendering of Edgar Allan Poe's "Annabel Lee" or Shakespeare's sonnet number twenty-nine: "When in disgrace with fortune and men's eyes / I all alone beweep my outcast state." Even those with only minimal education could sense and understand the import of an "outcast state" and its relevance to them. To me, this teacher was magic, and I wanted to be able, one day, to articulate with the artistry she possessed.

While our teachers and community leaders constantly reminded us that our public selves had to be projected in Standard English, I remember one incident where this was not so easily negotiated. I was a cheerleader for our high school football team, and we cheerleaders prided ourselves on the originality of our cheers. One of our favorites was, "Our boys gon' shine ta nite, our boys gon' shine, when the sun goes down and the moon comes up, our boys gon' shine." After one of our home games, my English teacher confronted me about my use of improper grammar in the cheer "gon' shine." We were, after all, in the public spotlight, she said, and we needed to put our best foot forward. I explained to her that I knew the grammar was "unofficial" but that "Our boys are going to shine tonight" would throw off the beat and just wouldn't work. That explanation didn't work, however, and we abandoned the cheer. Afterwards, she continued to monitor our on-field performances to make sure we didn't cross our languages and negatively reflect on our school and our teachers.

There were also specific times when the community reveled in the public use of Black English. One of these was during the celebration of the twentieth of May, the date when people in the Ocala area heard the news of the Emancipation Proclamation. The school was closed, and teachers, parents, ministers, deacons, and children gathered at the communal picnic grounds for baseball games, field races, card-playing, and barbecue. For such an occasion, the formal workday roles could be set aside, and the rhythmic ebb and flow of Black English dialect could be heard everywhere.

Many years later, I would become a scholar and professor of the Harlem Renaissance, that flowering of African-American literature and art in the 1920s and 1930s. I came to read the works of W. E. B. Du Bois, James Weldon Johnson, Alain Locke, and other key architects of the Renaissance who recognized that language cannot be separated from issues of power — and that language could be seized to create a "new" Negro. I came to read authors such as Zora Neale Hurston and Arna Bontemps, who helped shape the literary generations that followed: Toni Morrison, Gloria Naylor, Alice Walker, Toni Cade Bambara, to name a few. I studied the work of theorists such as Michel Foucault, who has observed the power of language to categorize, distribute, and manipulate those perceived as different from the majority. But in retrospect, much of this was not new. It was merely a continuation for me. Indeed, in Ocala, Florida, I learned my first — and most lasting — lessons about language, power, and identity.

My fascination with Black language stems from my father's enjoyment of absolute control over its manipulation. My father has mastered Black language rituals, certainly; he also has the ability to analyze them, to tell you what he is doing, why, and how. He is a very self-conscious language user. He is not atypical. It is amazing how much Black people in rituals such as barbershops and pool halls, street corners, and family reunions, talk about talking. Why do they do this? I think they do it to pass these rituals along from one generation to the next. They do it to preserve the traditions of "the race."

Henry Louis Gates, Jr.
The Signifying Monkey

Black English: Steppin Up? Lookin Back

BEVERLY JEAN SMITH

I may say honestly and truthfully that my one aim is and has always been so far as I may, to hold a torch for the children of a group too long exploited and too frequently disparaged in struggling for the light.

Anna Julia Cooper, teacher, scholar, writer, and activist in the Black Women's Club Movement

In my last seventeen years of public school teaching, I taught English at Brookline High School, a suburban high school because of its demographics and location. The student population was 3 percent Hispanic, 13 percent Asian, 11 percent African American, and 13 percent émigre. Fifty to sixty percent of the students were from divorced and single-parent households. Over sixty-four countries were represented, and almost every language in the world was spoken by its students. About 45 percent of the Black students and I lived in Roxbury, a predominantly African-American community of Boston, the adjoining major city. They participated in METCO, a voluntary busing program. During its thirty-five year transition from a nearly all-white school to its present diverse population, Brookline High has sustained its academic program, sending over 70 percent of each graduating class on to college.

During my tenure, a number of the Black students who resided in Roxbury used the expression *step up* to describe what they perceived as a disrespectful and challenging act towards them by one of their peers. A student would inform me, "If Wanda *steps up* to me, Imuh hafta beat her down." Why? Because being *stepped up* to is about how we want to be seen, how others see us, and how we see ourselves. Psychologist Susan Harter calls all this "seeing" self-esteem. To her, "self-esteem derives from two sources: how a person views her performance in areas in which success is important to her and how a person believes she is perceived by significant others, such as parents, teachers, or peers" (Feldman & Elliott, 1990).

Using this cultural context, I identify the negative reactions of those who opposed the resolution passed by the school board of the Oakland Unified School District as an example of *steppin up*. If young people's reality is shaped in part by their language, dismissing or devaluing how they talk is a way of disrespecting, of beginning to erase a part of who they are. As adults, you and I know a major rule that governs how people are expected to speak. If you want to be heard, you are to use your voice in ways the system feels are acceptable and appropriate. Avoid being loud, sound calm, and use Standard English. The unspoken rule, however, is that "appropriate voicing" and speaking Standard English well does not guarantee you will be heard.

My own experience and those of many of my Black friends and acquaintances confirm the latter. From boardrooms and courtrooms to classrooms, we Black Americans are emotionally and psychologically drained. In addition to not being heard, we spend extra energy trying to educate mostly middle-class white people who have minimal contact with Black communities or Black people about a reality different from the one they are living. Occasionally, they appear to understand what we are saying.

CODE-SWITCHING

If the truth be told, in the workplace, many of us fine upstanding mainstream professionals who speak Standard English well and who have spent years negotiating the terrain of a white middle-class norm speak Black English to maintain a sense of sanity, a sense of humor, and a sense of self. For example, my sister Donna, who teaches English in a Los Angeles high school with a predominantly white faculty, admits that sometimes in the middle of committee, department, or faculty meetings, she speaks Black English to extract herself from a discussion where she and everyone else is "using their best words." The code-switching "keeps me from goin crazy," she explains. It "reconnects [her] to self," to a Black vernacular that enables her to disrupt the competitive discourse and compels her colleagues to hear her voice. In no uncertain terms, she be tellin them that they been talkin jis to hear themselves talk and ain't said one thang about the real issue.

Similarly, Rep. Maxine Waters, (D-CA) recalls how Willie Brown and she would code-switch, begin speaking Black English to one another, in the midst of the legislative sessions in Sacramento. By speaking Black English, they were messing with their white colleagues' minds, reminding them that they still see themselves as being in kinship with the everyday Black folk who they also represent. They have not sold out their "kinfolk" and intend to hold their fellow politicians accountable. While these two politicians and my sister use Black English to encourage white people to do the right thing, Madeline Cartwright — a former principal of Blaine Elementary School — displays the beauty of Black English. She uses narrativizing, signifying, and call-response to elicit the support of the Black adults who were raising her students in a poverty-stricken area of Philadelphia.

In her autobiography *For the Children,* this principal describes her first parents' meeting.

> I am so happy to be here with you. I knew you were going to come so we could show our children that we are together, so you could know their principal and you could know their teachers. I am here to make this school serve the children. Now, I came from the same place as you. I told them about my childhood, about being the thirteenth of thirteen children, about living in a house with no beds, about sleeping on the floor, about moving into the projects when we left the country, about how we didn't have any shoes. I told them about my daddy chopping off those high heels [and making my brothers, sisters, and me wear them to school as flats]. They laughed so loud at that story I had to stop for a minute.

Then I said, I'm not from the Main Line. I *live* on the Main Line, but I've come up through the ranks. I have survived and beaten the odds to be standing up here tonight. Now, you must give me credit. I must have more sense than some of you, because I made it out and some of you are still here.

They loved that. They were laughing and nudging each other and having a good time, a comfortable time. I was dressed up, looking like new money, everything matching.

See these clothes? I bought this outfit yesterday for the show tonight. I'm not going to say to you that I'm ashamed I have this fancy outfit. I have ten more just like it at home. I am sorry that you don't have one. I wish you had one, too. But I have mine, and it looks goooood, doesn't it?

The room went wild, just bursting with laughter and cheers.

. . . Then, I went down into the crowd like a country preacher at a revival, pacing up and down the aisle, really putting on a show. Our teachers need to be respected. They must feel good about themselves too. Go home and tell your child that his teacher looked good tonight. Don't they look good? They may not look as good as *I* do , but they do look good, don't they?

By this time the teachers were laughing and clapping right along with the parents.

I want to be successful. But in order for me to be successful, the children must be successful. Success for any of us is success for all of us. The same with failure.

I love children, I really love children. But I need my paycheck, too. I get paid every two weeks if I keep this job, and the only way I will keep this job is if your children — *our* children — do well.

That Cadillac you saw parked out front, that belongs to me. It costs me two hundred and sixty-five dollars a month to keep it, and I can't pay for it without you. Will you help me pay for that car?"

The room burst into an ovation.

Are you telling me that I will be able to keep it?

The cheers and applause got even louder.

And that was it.

Amidst cheering and applause, I walked down the center aisle and into the foyer to personally greet my new congregation, who assured me that we were together — parents, teachers, and I — to serve the children. They told me how happy they were that I was their new principal. One tiny, elderly lady made her way over and took me aside.

"Honey," she said, patting me on the arm, "now don't you worry about a thing. We're going to help you to *pay* for that Cadillac." (Cartwright and D'Orso, 1993, pp. 105–106)

Enough said.

Outside of the workplace, we Black Americans gather, eat, "shoot the breeze," listen to music, play twist. Our words begin to sound like the language in the Black communities in which we were raised, which include Chicago, St. Louis, St. Augustine, Oakland, New York, and Boston. "I'll take a little of dis and a little of dat." "Must tis cuz must tain't don't sound right tuh me." I marvel at how Black English enables Black folks of my generation to be in relationship with each other, as a collective, in our birth, work, and adopted communities.

In retrospect, Black English abounds in the working-class Black communities in St. Louis and then, St. Charles, Missouri, where I grew up. Like many other Black baby boomers born between 1940 and 1950, I attended a segregated elementary school where Standard English ruled. We had spelling bees, conjugated verbs, and diagrammed sentences. Enunciation mattered. But, in the absence of teachers, Black English thrived. When the teacher stepped out of the room for a minute, we fifth-graders quieted ourselves in order to hear the males play the dozens, the first type of signifyin defined by Geneva Smitherman (see essay, page 29). I loved these outrageously creative one-on-one word duels.

First male: "Yo momma wear combat boots and concrete drawhs."

Second male: "Yo momma so ugly, she scare the white offuh rice."

First male: "Yo momma so ugly, when she run a bath, the water goes back up the faucet."

The second type of signifyin, "aimed at a person . . . for corrective criticism" (see Geneva Smitherman, page 29), I heard at recess or when we were walkin home from school. Two classic retorts, "If, you feel like froggy, JUMP on ovuhheruh" and "You bettuh-stop talkin sooomuch trash," advise individuals to start speaking or acting differently unless they want to end up in a fight. While we children used the second type, the adults in numerous Black communities raised such speech acts to an art form.

SIGNIFYIN LESSONS

These Black folks' way of signifyin taught me at least three lessons. One, I am accountable for my own behavior. Professing that my runnin buddies (gloss: friends) made me commit a particular act fell on deaf ears. "I know you know right from wrong." Two, I am always in relationship with my immediate and extended family/community. "You ain't grown, yet" served as a reminder that I was not free to do as I pleased, especially if I was still livin under their roof (gloss: in a family member's home). Adults in hearing distance thought nothing of put'n me or my friends in check (gloss: letting us know they disapproved of our behavior so correct it). All they needed to say is "I know, I didn't hear, what I thought I heard, cumin outta yo mouf." Black folks in the community and who taught us in school took for granted that we Black children had good home training. So, if our behavior reflected otherwise, with conviction our school teachers proclaimed, "I know your mother taught you better." The community expected us to honor what we had been taught.

The third lesson was, read between the lines, exercise reason and, if the opportunity exists to save yourself, do so. My mother's signifyin taught my older sister Donna and me this profound lesson. Using soft, calm, and measured speech, our mother would tell us, "This is the last time I'm gown to talk to you about this. You understand me." Or, she would implore us, "Please, don't y'all make me haveta git up and cum in there."

And although I heard my mother say a many a time, "I'm bout two seconds offa yo behind," I only remember my mother hitting me twice.

These were never idle threats but her way of giving us an opportunity to stop all that foolishness and redeem ourselves. We realized that our actions influenced how we would be treated by her and ultimately others. Her faith in us to start acting like we had good sense compelled us to think about the consequences if we continued doing whatever we might be doing. Though my mother certainly did signify, she never ever hollered at us. We felt respected and valued. With youth, my mother and other Black grown-ups used the second type of signifyin as a language of development. They used it to convey community and family expectations rather than to humiliate or guilt. They used it to freeze frame or cause us to pause in a way that invited us to monitor our own behavior.

Looking back has made me realize, in twenty-three years of teaching mostly white adolescents from middle– and upper-middle class families, how much my own classroom practice and interactions with all of my students were informed by a mindset Black English helped shape. I always gave my students a chance to correct their own behavior. If they didn't, I might say one of the following: "*I know you know bettuh.*" "*Don't make me act ugly.*" "*People, you're pressin your luck.*" "*I don't miss nothin that goes on in this class room. I'm jis givin you a chance to straighten up.*" After awhile, my students commented that I used "funny expressions." They were right and I rarely had major discipline problems.

I try never to *step up* to youth. Whether I teach, spend time with them, or simply pass youth on the street, I try to make expectations clear and let them know I respect and value them. For example, a neighbor's son and his friend pulled up in front of our building. The son left the car running and ran inside. A hip hop song containing profanity began blaring out of the car. I look at his friend, whom I had never met, and said, "Sweetheart, please turn the music down. This is a public street." He replied, "No, problem," and reduced the volume. This is the legacy left to me by the Black adults in my family and community, whose use of Black English cultivated a way of being.

In mainstream society, *stepping up* has a positive connotation. It means to emerge as a leader, to fill a void in a positive way. The school board of the Oakland Unified School District stepped up, big time. It put forth a resolution to heighten awareness, to serve notice that Black English is not the problem but a possible resource. Other school systems and schools of education need to follow Oakland's lead. Teachers need resources and knowledge that will help them better understand the structure and characteristics of Black English so they can show students who speak it and do not know how to code-switch how to do so. The latter should enable students to be more facile with Standard English, access knowledge, have choices, and achieve some measure of success. The school board of the Oakland Unified School District seems to understand that providing an equitable educational environment for students who our schools presently underserve is serious bizness that demands bold strides, rather than half-steppin.

Resources on Ebonics

Recommendations from Theresa Perry

SMITHERMAN, GENEVA. (1986). *Talkin and Testifyin: The Language of Black America.* Detroit: Wayne State University Press. This wonderful book is still the best introduction to the study of Black Language available. It is required reading for teachers who work with African-American children.

GATES, HENRY LOUIS, JR., & McKAY, NELLIE V. (Eds.). (1997). *The Norton Anthology of African American Literature.* Too many teachers have never read African-American literature. Those who have read individual works have not systematically explored the tradition and come to understand how it draws upon the vernacular language of African Americans. This anthology is where teachers who work with African-American children can find direction in their study of the African-American literary tradition.

HOOVER, MARY RHODES. (1996). *Super Literacy.* Benicia, CA: Onyx Publishing Co. *Super Literacy* is a fast-paced, multifaceted curriculum/methodology for teaching reading, writing, and speaking to African-American students and other students for whom English is not their first language. This phonics-inclusive approach to literacy is based on the premise that no singular methodology will develop the high level of literacy skills that African Americans want for their children. It emphasizes multiple approaches to developing fluency in reading, writing, and speaking, including daily affirmations, oratory, literature, linguistic-based phonics instruction, content area reading, comprehension, test-taking activities, and memorization. These curriculum materials were initially developed by Mary Rhodes Hoover for the Nairobi School almost thirty years ago, and they have been used in school systems around the country. They were recently used as part of the Standard English Proficiency program in Oakland. Mary Rhodes Hoover is a professor of education at Howard University who specializes in African-American language and literacy. She is available for consultations and can be reached at Howard University, School of Education, 2441 Fourth St., NW, Room 132, Washington, DC 20059. 202–806–7343.

Recommendations from Wayne O'Neil

Let me recommend not books but the following two quite different types of material for teachers to look at:

1. For more discussion of the Ebonics issue from the point of view of linguists and expanding on the issues raised in my article, I suggest: a) Pullem, Geoffrey. (1997, March 27). Language That Dare Not Speak Its Name. *Nature*, 321–322. b) The Linguistic Society of America. Resolution on the "Ebonics" Issue. (See pages 143–147.) c) Fillmore, Charles. A Linguist Looks at the Ebonics Debate. At: http://parents.berkeley.edu/current/ebonics.html

2. But to get an understanding of the madness out there on this issue and the sometimes frightening racist energy spent on it, I recommend that teachers turn to the Internet, do an "Ebonics" Web search, and thus get a sense of how important it is to bring the Ebonics/Black English/African-American English issue into the realm of rational discussion, for it is likely that their students are seeing the Web material and its racism, misinformation, and miseducation.

Recommendations from Mary Rhodes Hoover

DELPIT, LISA. (1995). *Other People's Children: Cultural Conflict in the Classroom*. New York: New Press. Gives an excellent background on issues related to language and literacy.

HOOVER, MARY, DABNEY, N, & LEWIS, S. (1990). *Successful Black and Minority Schools.* San Francisco: Julian Richardson. Describes successful literacy programs, where students test at and above grade level, for Ebonics speakers.

I would also recommend Geneva Smitherman's *Talkin and Testifyin: The Language of Black America (1986),* which remains the best summary of African-American Language/Ebonics.

Recommendations from Terry Meier

DANDY, EVELYN. (1991). *Black Communications: Breaking Down the Barriers.* Chicago: African American Images. For teachers and future teachers, Dandy's book provides a great introduction to the topic of Black Language/Ebonics. She includes many classroom examples that teachers can relate to easily and that spark much discussion about effective teaching practice.

I would also recommend, as others have, Lisa Delpit's *Other People's Children: Cultural Conflict in the Classroom* (1995) and Geneva Smitherman's *Talkin and Testifyin: The Language of Black America* (1986).

Recommendations from Rethinking Schools

Rethinking Schools is the country's leading grassroots journal for reform of our public schools. Subscriptions are $12.50/year. Contact *Rethinking Schools,* 1001 E. Keefe Ave., Milwaukee, WI 53212. Call toll-free 1–800–669–4192. Explore the Ebonics debate on its Web page: www.rethinking schools.org.

Clarifying Terminology

Following are definitions of some of the terms used in the debate on Ebonics. The definitions are based on the most commonly accepted usage of the term in linguistics and educational literature.

AFRICAN-AMERICAN VERNACULAR TRADITION: "In African American literature, the vernacular refers to the church songs, blues, ballads, sermons, stories, and in our own era, rap songs that are part of the oral tradition; not primarily the literature (or written-down) tradition of Black expression. . . . What would the work of Langston Hughes, Sterling Brown, Zora Neale Hurston, and Ralph Ellison be like without its Black vernacular ingredients? What for that matter would the writings of Mark Twain or William Faulkner be without those same elements? Still this material also has its own shape, its own integrity, its own place in the Black literary canon: the literature of the vernacular." Gates, H. L., Jr., & McKay, N. V. (Eds.). (1997). *The Norton Anthology of African American Literature*. New York: Norton.

BLACK ENGLISH: A dialect of English, spoken by descendants of enslaved Africans in the United States, which has its own grammar and rules of discourse.

DIALECT: "A regionally or socially distinctive variety of a language, identified by a particular set of words and grammatical structures . . . . One dialect may predominate as the official or standard form of the language, and this is the variety which may come to be written down." Crystal, D. (Ed.). *A Dictionary of Linguistics and Phonetics* (4th ed.). (p. 114). Malden, MA: Blackwell.

EBONICS/BLACK LANGUAGE/AFRICAN-AMERICAN LANGUAGE: "Linguistic and paralinguistic features which on a concentric continuum represent the communicative competence of the West African, Caribbean, and United States slave descendants of African origin." Williams, R. L. (1975). *Ebonics: The True Language of Black Folks.* St. Louis: Institute of Black Studies. See also the essay by Ernie Smith, page 49, in which he notes that in the hybridization process of English and African languages, it was the grammar of the Niger-Congo African languages that was dominant, and that the extensive word borrowing from the English stock does not make Ebonics a dialect of English. Smith also notes that Eurocentric scholars "lack any logical reasons for using vocabulary as their basis for classifying Black American speech, while using grammar as their basis for classifying English."

SLANG: "The nonstandard vocabulary of a given culture." O'Neil, W. (1997). If Ebonics Isn't a Language, Then Tell Me, What Is? See page 38.

STANDARD BLACK ENGLISH: "[Has] the grammar of standardized, textbook, or educated English and phonology which is less like that of [Ebonics] . . . but with intonational patterns that in some way identify the speaker as Black. . . . Standard Black English is identical [except for stylistic features] to other written standard speech varieties, while spoken SBE often identifies the speaker as Black. "Lewis, S. (1981). Practical Aspects of Teaching Composition to Bidialectical Students: The Narrative Methods. In M. Whiteman (Ed.), *Writing: The Narrative, Development, and Teaching of Written Communication.* Hillsdale, NJ: Lawrence Erlbaum.

STANDARD ENGLISH: "[T]he variety which forms the basis of printed English in newspapers and books, which is used in the mass media and which is taught in school . . . ." Yule, G. (1996). *The Study of Language* (2nd ed.). (p. 277). Cambridge, Eng.: Cambridge University Press.

VERNACULAR: "[Refers] to the indigenous language . . . of a speech community, e.g., the vernacular of Liverpool, Berkshire, Jamaica, etc. . . . Vernaculars are usually seen in contrast to such notions as standard, lingua franca. . . ." Crystal, D. (Ed.). *A Dictionary of Linguistics and Phonetics* (4th ed.). (pp. 410–411). Malden, MA: Blackwell.

Notes and References

Theresa Perry, pages 3–16

References

ANDERSON, J. (1988). *The Education of Blacks in the South, 1800–1935.* (Chapel Hill: University of North Carolina Press.

CORNELIUS, J. D. (1991). *When I Can Read My Title Clear.* Columbia: University of South Carolina Press.

GATES, H. L., JR. (1991). Bearing Witness. In H. L. Gates, Jr. (Ed.), *Selections of African American Autobiography in the Twentieth Century.* New York: Pantheon.

LISCHER, R. (1995). *The Preacher King: Martin Luther King, Jr. and the Word that Moved America.* New York: Oxford University Press.

MORRISON, T. (1997). The Official Story: Dead Man Golfing. In T. Morrison and C. Brodsky Lacour (Eds.), *Birth of a Nation'hood: Gaze, Script and Spectacle in the O. J. Simpson Case.* New York: Pantheon.

PERRY, T. (1996). Situating Malcolm X in the African American Narrative Tradition: Freedom for Literacy and Literacy for Freedom. In T. Perry (Ed.), *Teaching Malcolm X.* New York: Routledge.

ROEDIGER, D. (1991). *The Wages of Whiteness.* London, New York: Verso.

SHAW, S. (1996). *What a Woman Ought to Be and to Do: Black Professional Women During the Jim Crow Era.* Chicago: University of Chicago Press.

STEPTOE, W. (1979). *From Behind the Veil: A Study of Afro-American Narrative.* Urbana: University of Illinois Press.

X, MALCOLM. (1987). *The Autobiography of Malcolm X.* New York: Ballantine.

Notes

1. One of the most serious theoretical flaws embedded in most conversations about multicultural education and changing demographics is the assumption that all people of color in this country are similarly situated politically and that their cultural formations carry similar political salience. The school performance of African Americans in minority/majority school districts should compel us to inject the notion of "a racial caste group" into discussions of multiculturalism in schools, in the workplace, and in the economic order.

2. From the very beginning, the Black press — *Essence, Emerge, The Chicago Defender, The Amsterdam News,* the *Bay State Banner* — were more balanced in their coverage, including articles for and against the resolution.

3. bell hooks, Marva Perry, and Nancy Hughes are African Americans who grew up and were educated, at least until the eighth grade, in southern segregated Black schools. bell hooks is a noted feminist scholar and author; Marva Perry is a clinician and vice president for student development at Wheelock College; Nancy Hughes is an accomplished writer and teacher who has her own film production company in Boston.

Lisa Delpit, pages 17–26

References

BERDAN, R. (1980). Knowledge into Practice: Delivering Research to Teachers. In M. F. Whiteman (Ed.), *Reactions to Ann Arbor: Vernacular Black English and Education.* Arlington, VA: Center for Applied Linguistics.

BRICE HEATH, S. (1983). *Ways with Words.* Cambridge, Eng.: Cambridge University Press.

CAZDEN, C. B. (1988). *Classroom Discourse.* Portsmouth, NH: Heinemann.

CUNNINGHAM, P. M. (1976–1977). Teachers' Correction Responses to Black-Dialect Miscues Which Are Nonmeaning-Changing. *Reading Research Quarterly 12.*

MICHAELS, S. & CAZDEN, C. B. (1986). Teacher-Child Collaboration on

Oral Preparation for Literacy. In B. Schieffer (Ed.), *Acquisition of Literacy: Ethnographic Perspectives.* Norwood, NJ: Ablex.

NELSON-BARBER, S. (1982). Phonologic Variations of Pima English. In R. St. Clair and W. Leap (Eds.), *Language Renewal Among American Indian Tribes: Issues, Problems and Prospects.* Rosslyn, VA: National Clearinghouse for Bilingual Education.

SIMS, R. (1982) Dialect and Reading: Toward Redefining the Issues. In J. Langer and M. T. Smith-Burke (Eds.), *Reader Meets Author/Bridging the Gap.* Newark, DE: International Reading Asssociation.

Note

1. Some of these books include Lucille Clifton, *All Us Come 'Cross the Water* (New York: Holt, Rinehart, and Winston, 1973); Paul Green (aided by Abbe Abbott), *I Am Eskimo — Aknik My Name* (Juneau: Alaska Northwest Publishing, 1959); Howard Jacobs and Jim Rice, *Once upon a Bayou* (New Orleans: Phideaux Publications, 1983); Tim Elder, *Santa's Cajun Christmas Adventure* (Baton Rouge: Little Cajun Books, 1981); and a series of biographies produced by Yukon-Koyukkuk School District of Alaska and published by Hancock House Publishers in North Vancouver, British Columbia, Canada.

Geneva Smitherman, pages 29–37

References

ANGELOU, M. (1971). *Just Give Me a Cool Drink of Water 'fore I Die.* New York: Random House.

FANON, F. (1967). The Negro and Language. In *Black Skin, White Masks.* New York: Grove Press.

FREIRE, P. (1985). *The Politics of Education: Culture, Power, and Liberation* (D. Macedo, Trans.). Massachusetts: Bergin & Garvey Publishers, now an imprint of Greenwood Publishing Group, Westport, CT.

SMITHERMAN, G. (1977, 1986). *Talkin and Testifyin: The Language of Black America.* Detroit: Wayne State University Press.

SMITHERMAN, G. (1995). Introduction. In J. Percelay, S. Dweck, and M. Ivey, *Double Snaps.* New York: William Morrow.

SPEARS, A. K. (1982). The Black English Semi-Auxiliary Come. *Language* 58(4), 850–872.

TROUTMAN-ROBINSON, D., & SMITHERMAN, G. (1997). Discourse as Social Interaction. In T. A. van Dijk (Ed.), *Discourse, Ethnicity, Culture, and Racism.* (pp. 144–180). London: Sage Publications.

WILLIAMS, R. L. (Ed.). (1975). *Ebonics: The True Language of Black Folks.* St. Louis: Institute of Black Studies.

Ernie Smith, pages 49–58

References

ALLEYNE, M. (1971). Linguistic Continuity of Africa in the Caribbean. In R. J. Henry (Ed.), *Topics in Afro-American Studies.* (p. 125). New York: Black Academy Press.

BLACKSHIRE-BELAY, C. A. (1996). The Location of Ebonics Within the Framework of the Africological Paradigm. *Journal of Black Studies 27,* 5–23.

BROSNAHAN, L. F., & MALMBERG, B. (1970). *Introduction to Phonetics.* Cambridge, Eng.: Cambridge University Press.

CHAMBERS, J., JR. (Ed.). (1983). *Black English: Educational Equity and the Law.* Ann Arbor: Karoma.

CROZIER, K. (1996). *Instructional Programs Designed to Teach Standard English to African American Elementary Students.* Unpublished master's thesis, California State University — Fresno.

DEFRANTZ, A. (1975). *A Critique of the Literature on Black English.* Michigan: University Microfilms International.

DILLARD, J. L. (1972). *Black English — Its History and Usage in the United States.* New York: Vintage.

DUNCAN, G. X. (1995). Langue, Parole and the Nature of Culture: Toward a Progressive Pedagogy of Language and Literacy for Speakers of Ebonics (Black Language). In M. A. Ice and M. A. Saunders Lucas (Eds.), *Reading: The Blending of Theory and Practice Seventh Annual Reading Conference Year Book 3.* (pp. 49–68). Bakersfield: California State University.

HARE, N. (1965). *Black Anglo Saxons.* Chicago: Third World Press.

HARRISON, D. S., & TRABASSO, T. (Eds.). (1976). *Black English: A Seminar.* New York: John Wiley & Sons.

HERSKOVITS, M. (1941, 1958). *Myth of the Negro Past.* Boston: Beacon Press.

JAHN, J. (1961). *Muntu: An Outline of the New African Culture.* (p. 194). New York: Grove Press.

JOINER, C., JUDGE. (1979). *Memorandum Opinion and Order* Detroit: United States District Court.

LADEFOGED, P. (1968). *A Phonetic Study of West African Languages.* Cambridge, Eng.: Cambridge University Press.

MERRIWHETHER, L., & DOVE, A. (1967, December 9). Soul Folks Chittlin Test. *Jet Magazine.*

O'GRADY, W., DOBROVOSKY, M., & ARNOFF, M. (1993). *Contemporary Linguistics: An Introduction.* New York: St. Martin's Press.

PALMER, L. R. (1978). *Descriptive and Comparative Linguistics: A Critical Introduction.* London: Faber and Faber Limited.

ROMAINE, S. (1994). *Language and Society: An Introduction to Sociolinguistics.* Oxford, Eng.: Oxford University Press.

SMITH, E. (1974). *The Evolution and Continuing Presence of the African Oral Tradition in Black America.* Unpublished doctoral dissertation, University of California — Irvine.

SMITHERMAN, G. (1977, 1986). *Talkin and Testifying: The Language of Black America.* Detroit: Wayne State University Press.

STOLLER, P. (Ed.). (1975). *Black American English: Its Background and Its Usage in the Schools and in Literature.* New York: Dell.

TURNER, L. D. (1973). *Africanisms in the Gullah Dialect.* Ann Arbor: University of Michigan Press.

TWIGGS, R. (1973). *Pan African Language in the Western Hemisphere.* Quincy MA: Christopher.

WEDDINGTON, G. T. (Ed.), (1979, June). *Journal of Black Studies 9,* 4.

WELMERS, W. E. (1973). *African Language Structures.* Berkeley: University of California Press.

WILLIAMS, R. L. (1975). *Ebonics: The True Language of Black Folks.* St. Louis: Institute of Black Studies.

WILLIAMSON, J. (1969). A Look at Black English. *Journal of Educational Psychology*, 169–185.

WOODSON, C. G. (1933). *Mis-Education of the Negro.* Washington D.C.: The Associated Publishers.

Mary Rhodes Hoover, pages 71–76

References

ASANTE, M. (1990). African Elements in African American English. In J. Holloway (Ed.), *Africanisms in American Culture.* Bloomington: Indiana University Press.

BAUGH, J. (183). *Black Street Speech.* Austin: University of Texas Press.

BAZELY, M. (1996, December 22). Ebonics: Self-Worth at Heart of Issue. *The Oakland Tribune.*

BROWN, S. (1933). Negro Character as Seen by White Authors. *Journal of Negro Education 2,* 179–203.

CHALL, J. (1967). *Learning to Read: The Great Debate.* New York: McGraw Hill.

DELPIT, L. (1995). *Other People's Children: Cultural Conflict in the Classroom.* New York: New Press.

FOORMAN, B. R., ET. AL. (1996, May 4). Early Intervention for Children with Reading Problems: Study Designs and Preliminary Findings. Cited in R. Colvin, Phonics Is Best Aid For Reading, Study Shows. *Los Angeles Times,* pp. A1, A20.

HOOVER, M. R., DABNEY, N., & LEWIS, S. (Eds.). (1990). *Successful Black and Minority Schools.* San Francisco: Julian Richardson.

HOOVER, M. R., LEWIS, S. A. R., POLITZER, R. L., FORD, J., McNAIR-KNOX, F., HICKS, S., & WILLIAMS, D. (1996). Tests of African American English for Teachers of Bidialectical Students. In R. L. Jones (Ed.), *Handbook of Tests and Measurements for Black Populations.* Hampton, VA: Cobb & Henry.

HOOVER, M. R., McNAIR-KNOX, F., LEWIS, S. A. R., & POLITZER, R. L. (1996). African American English Attitude Measures for Teachers. In R. L. Jones (Ed.), *Handbook of Tests and Measurements for Black Populations,* vol. 1. Hampton, VA: Cobb & Henry.

HOOVER, M. R., POLITZER, R. L., BROWN, D., LEWIS, S. A. R. HICKS, S., & McNAIR-KNOX, F. (1996). African American English Tests for Students. In R. L. Jones (Ed.), *Handbook of Tests and Measurements for Black Populations*. Hampton, VA: Cobb & Henry.

HYMES, D. (1972). Toward Ethnographies of Communication: The Analysis of Communicative Events. In P. Giglioli (Ed.), *Language and Social Context*. Baltimore: Penguin.

JONES, R. L. (Ed.). *Handbook of Tests and Measurements for Black Populations*. Hampton, VA: Cobb & Henry.

ROSE, T. (1994). *Black Noise: Rap Music and Black Culture in Contemporary America*. Hanover: University Press of New England.

SMITH, E. (1974). The Evolution and Continuing Presence of the African Oral Tradition in America. Unpublished doctoral dissertation, University of California — Irvine.

SMITHERMAN, G. (1977, 1986). *Talkin' and Testifyin: The Language of Black America*. Detroit: Wayne State University Press.

TAYLOR, O., & MATSUDA, M. (1988). Storytelling and Classroom Discrimination. In G. Smitherman & T. A. van Dijk (Eds.), *Discourse and Discrimination*. Detroit: Wayne State University Press.

TURNER, L. (1969). *Africanisms in the Gullah Dialect*. New York: Arno Press.

Terry Meier, pages 94–103

References

GATES, H. L., JR. (1990). The Master's Pieces: On Canon Formation and the Afro-American Tradition. In C. Moran and E. F. Penfield (Eds.), *Conversation: Contemporary Critical Theory and the Teaching of Literature*. Urbana, IL: National Council of Teachers of English.

LeCLAIR, T. (1981, March 21). "The Language Must Not Sweat": A Conversation with Toni Morrison. *The New Republic*, p. 27.

LEWIS, S. A. (1981). Practical Aspects of Teaching Composition to Bidialectal Students: The Nairobi Method. In M. F. Whiteman (Ed.), *Writing: The Nature, Development, and Teaching of Written Composition*. Hillsdale, NJ: Lawrence Erlbaum.

MARSHALL, P. (1983). *From the Poets in the Kitchen.* New York: Feminist Press.

McKISSACK, P. (1986). *Flossie and the Fox.* New York: Dutton.

SHANGE, N. (1975). toussaint. In *For Colored Girls Who Have Considered Suicide When the Rainbow is Enuf.* New York: Collier.

SMITHERMAN, G. (1973, May–June). White English in Blackface, Or Who Do I Be? *The Black Scholar.*

Terry Meier, pages 117–125

References

BRICE HEATH, S. (1983). *Ways with Words.* New York: Cambridge University Press.

GOODWIN, M. H. (1990). *He-Said-She-Said: Talk as Social Organization among Black Children.* Bloomington: Indiana University Press.

HALE-BENSON, J. (1982). *Black Children: Their Roots, Culture and Learning Styles.* New York: Johns Hopkins University Press.

LABOV, W. (1972). *Language in the Inner City: Studies in the Black English Vernacular.* Philadelphia: University of Pennsylvania Press.

TAYLOR, D., & DORSEY-GAINES, C. (1988). *Growing Up Literate.* London: Heineman.

VERNON-FEAGANS, L. (1996). *Children's Talk in Communities and Classrooms.* Cambridge: Blackwell Publishers.

Mary Rhodes Hoover, pages 126–133

References

ALLEYNE, M. (1980). *Comparative Afro-American.* Ann Arbor, MI: Karoma.

CARROL, J. (1972). Defining Language Comprehension; Some Speculations. In Freedle and Carrol (Eds.), *Language Comprehension and the Acquisition of Knowledge.* Washington, D.C.: V. H. Winston, distributed by Halston Press. Division of Wiley, New York.

EKWALL, E., & SHANKER, J. (1993). *Reading Inventory.* Boston: Allyn & Bacon.

FASOLD, R. (1972, April 27). Sloppy Speech in Standard English. Paper read at the Fourth Triennial Conference on Symbolic Processes. Washington, D.C.

HILLIARD, A. (1992). *Testing African American Students.* Morristown, NJ: Aaron.

HOOVER, M. R. (1984, April). Teacher Competency Tests . . . The Florida Teacher Certification Examination. *Negro Educational Review, 35*(2), 70–77.

HOOVER, M. R. (1987). Black Education in Crisis: Standardized Testing and Miseducation. *National Black Law Journal, 10*(1), 25–27.

HOOVER, M. R. (1992, Spring). The Nairobi Day School: An African American Independent School, 1966–1984. *Journal of Negro Education, 61*(2),201–210.

HOOVER, M. R., DABNEY, N., & LEWIS, S. A. R. (1990). *Successful Black and Minority Schools.* San Francisco: Julian Richardson.

HOOVER, M. R., DANIELS, D., & LEWIS, S., ET AL. (1989). *The One-Two-Three Method: A Writing Process for Bidialectal Students.* Edina, MN: Bellweather Press.

HOOVER, M. R., & POLITZER, R. (1982). A Culturally Appropriate Composition Assessment: The Nairobi Method. In M. Whiteman (Ed.), *Variations in Writing: Functional and Linguistic-Cultural Differences.* Hilldale, NJ: Lawrence Ehrlbaum.

HOOVER, M. R., POLITZER, R. L., BROWN, D., LEWIS, S. A. R., HICKS, S., & McNAIR-KNOX, F. (1996). African American English Tests for Students. In R. L. Jones (Ed.), *Handbook of Tests and Measures for Black Populations.* Hampton, VA: Cobb & Henry.

HOOVER, M. R., POLITZER, R., & TAYLOR, O. (1991). Bias in Reading Tests for Black Language Speakers: A Sociolinguistic Perspective. In A. Hilyard (Ed.), *Testing African American Students.* Morristown, NJ: Aaron.

NEILL, M. (1996, February). Assessment Reform at a Crossroads. *Education Week.*

ORTONY, A., ET AL. (1985). Cultural and Instructional Influences on Figurative Language Comprehension by Inner City Children. *Research in the Teaching of English, 19,* 5–36.

SCHONEMANN, J. (1987). An Experimental, Exploratory Study of Causes of Bias in Test Items. *Journal of Educational Measurements, 24*(2), 97–118.

SMITHERMAN, G. (1977, 1986). *Talkin and Testifyin.* Detroit: Wayne State University Press.

WEINSTEIN, M. (1997, October 11). *The Bell Curve* Revisited by Scholars. *New York Times,* p. A22.

WHITE. (1992). *Selected Writings on Testing, 1978–1992.* Berkeley, CA: Testing for the Public.

WILEY, E. (1990, March). Biased Textbooks and Exams Cultivating Illiterate Minority Population. *Black Issues in Higher Education.*

WILKS, G. (1990). Nairobi Schools. In M. R. Hoover (Ed.), *Successful Black and Minority Schools.* San Francisco: Julian Richardson.

Monique Brinson, pages 134–139

References

DELPIT, L. (1995). *Other People's Children.* New York: New Press.

JACOBSEN, D., EGGEN, P., & KAUCHAK, D. (1989). *Methods for Teaching: A Skills Approach.* New York: Macmillan.

KOZOL, J. (1991). *Savage Inequalities: Children in America's Schools.* New York: Crown.

WAGSTAFF, J. (1994). *Phonics That Work: New Strategies for the Reading/ Writing Classroom.* New York: Scholastic.

Beverly Jean Smith, pages 197–204

References

CARTWRIGHT, M., & D'ORSO, D. (1993). *For the Children: Lessons from a Visionary Principal.* New York: Doubleday.

HARTER, S. (1990). Self and Identity Development. In S. Feldman and G. Elliott (Eds.), *At the Threshold: The Developing Adolescent.* Cambridge, MA: Harvard University Press.

Contributors

An acclaimed writer of fiction, drama, and essays, JAMES BALDWIN (1924–1987) was born in Harlem. His major works include the novels *Go Tell It on the Mountain* (1953) and *Giovanni's Room* (1956) as well as an autobiography, *Notes of a Native Son* (1955). His essay in this volume first appeared as a letter to the editor in the *New York Times* in 1979. It was written in response to the reaction to the "Black English" case, a federal court order affirming the legitimacy of Black English and mandating appropriate instruction for African-American children to acquire Standard English.

MONIQUE BRINSON teaches first and second grade in Roxbury, part of the city of Boston. She attended Boston College and graduated with a masters in education from Wheelock College Graduate School. She has been a cooperating teacher for ten graduate and five undergraduate students from local colleges throughout the Boston area.

TONI COOK has served on the Oakland school board since 1990. It was Cook who prodded her fellow trustees on the board to unanimously support the nation's first education policy recognizing Ebonics as the "primary language" of many students, comparing their language needs with those of immigrant children.

HAFEEZAH ADAMADAVIA DALJI is a high school English teacher in the Oakland public schools. Dalji was the first African-American woman to head the English department at Castlemont, one of the largest high schools in Oakland. She is also national vice president of the National Association of Black Reading and Language Development.

LISA DELPIT is holder of the Benjamin E. Mays Chair of Urban Educational Excellence at Georgia State University in Atlanta. A former Mac-

Arthur fellow, her most recent book is *Other People's Children: Cultural Conflict in the Classroom* (1995).

CAROLYN GETRIDGE was the Oakland superintendent of schools when the Ebonics policy passed; in the summer of 1997 she took a job in the private sector.

MARY RHODES HOOVER is a professor in the school of education at Howard University. She is a literacy consultant to the Oakland school district's Standard English Proficiency program (SEP) and the author of over thirty research articles on Black Language and literacy.

TERRY MEIER is an associate professor in the Wheelock College Graduate School in Boston.

BARBARA MINER is the managing editor of *Rethinking Schools*, an urban educational journal, and coeditor of *Rethinking Our Classrooms, Funding for Justice*, and *Selling Out Our Schools*.

WAYNE O'NEIL is head of the department of linguistics and philosophy at the Massachusetts Institute of Technology.

THERESA PERRY is vice president for community relations and associate professor of education at Wheelock College in Boston. She is editor of *Teaching Malcolm X* (1996) and co-editor with James Fraser of *Freedom's Plow: Teaching in the Multicultural Classroom* (1993).

JOHN RICKFORD, a linguistics professor at Stanford University since 1980, was born in Georgetown, Guyana, and received his doctorate in linguistics from the University of Pennsylvania. For the past twenty-five years, he has focused on the relationship between language and culture, developing models that use sociology, anthropology, and linguistics to explain and resolve educational problems. He is currently co-authoring a book on Ebonics, *African-American Vernacular English*, and co-editing three other books.

JOYCE HOPE SCOTT is associate professor of English and American literature at Massachusetts Maritime College and adjunct professor of African and African-American literature at Wheelock College in Boston. Her current projects include a volume of critical essays on gender, literature, and cultural nationalisms and essays on the literature of countries of the African Sahel.

Carrie Secret is a fifth-grade teacher at Prescott Elementary School, the only school in the Oakland Unified School District where a majority of the teachers voluntarily agreed to adopt the Standard English Proficiency program (SEP).

Beverly Jean Smith, a published poet, is assistant professor of education at Lesley College in Boston and a former chairperson of the *Harvard Educational Review.* She would like to acknowledge the contributions of her sister Donna and the friends who have informed her writing.

Ernie Smith is professor of medicine and clinical linguistics at Charles R. Drew University of Medicine and Science in Los Angeles. Dr. Smith was a consultant to the Oakland school district's Standard English Proficiency program (SEP).

Geneva Smitherman is University Distinguished Professor of English and Director of the African-American Language and Literacy Program at Michigan State University. From 1977–1979, she was the chief advocate and expert witness for the children in *King* (the "Black English" federal court case). She is the author of eight books and over one hundred articles and papers on the language, culture, and education of African Americans, most notably the classic work, *Talkin and Testifyin: The Language of Black America* (1977, rev. 1986), and *Black Talk: Words and Phrases from the Hood to the Amen Corner* (1994).

Isaac Taggert is co-founder and co-chair of the Oakland community group Africans United for Self-Help. He was a member of the Task Force on Educating African-American students that, as part of a broader program of school reform for the Oakland public schools, recommended what became known as the Ebonics resolution.

Credits

Acknowledgments

The editors would like to thank Robert Lowe, one of the founders and a former board member of *Rethinking Schools*, for bringing to the board the idea of a special issue on the Ebonics Debate. From the very beginning, Bob saw how important it was for the "Ebonics issue" to be framed, discussed, and debated by African-American educators, scholars, and activist.

From this project's inception to the completion of the book, Nancy Hutchins, Executive Assistant in the Undergraduate Division Office at Wheelock College, and Theela McCormick, Administrative Assistant in the Center for Urban Educational Excellence, have provided intelligent, diligent, and invaluable support. We thank them for their unusual generosity.

We are deeply grateful to the *Rethinking Schools* board for breaking with tradition and providing space — a whole issue — where Ebonics could be thoughtfully discussed, and also for handing over to us the editorship of the special issue.

It is hard to adequately express the important and central role played by Barbara Miner, Managing Editor of *Rethinking Schools*, in the development and completion of this project. Barbara doggedly and brilliantly managed the production of the special issue. She copyedited each of the entries such that the individual voices were not rendered as a monotone, but were able to retain their unique timbre, style, and nuance. She also made wonderful suggestions, and in such a manner that you were always disposed to stand up and take notice. In truth, she was the third editor.

Many thanks to Andy Hrycyna and Tisha Hooks, who shepherded this book through the Beacon Press process, and who with great sensitivity, care and integrity worked closely with *Rethinking Schools* to make this collaborative publishing project a reality.

Finally, a special note of thanks to the African-American community in Oakland, California, who stood up for our children.

Rethinking Schools is a nonprofit publisher advocating the reform of elementary and secondary public schools, with a special focus on equity and social justice. It began in Milwaukee in 1986 as a quarterly journal edited by teachers and educators who wanted to help organize a movement to reform public schools in Milwaukee. Over the years, *Rethinking Schools* has broadened its focus to include national concerns and to publish both the journal and special publications. Its fundamental mission has not changed, however. It still believes that public schools, in particular urban schools, must be reformed to meet the needs of all children. It still believes public schools are fundamental to the creation of a humane, caring, multiracial democracy. *Rethinking Schools'* publications emphasize actual classroom practice — the day-to-day realities faced by teachers, parents, and students — and the importance of equitable education opportunities. In its curriculum resources, it weaves issues of academic excellence, equity, and social justice into the life of the classroom. In its policy resources, it produces articles on key topics ranging from vouchers to standards, in day-to-day language accessible to all. In addition to the quarterly journal, special publications range from *Rethinking Our Classroom: Teaching for Equity and Justice* to *Selling Out Our Schools: Vouchers, Markets, and the Future of Public Education* to *Rethinking Columbus: Teaching about Columbus's Arrival in America.* Subscriptions are $12.50/year. For a free catalog contact *Rethinking Schools*, 1001 E. Keefe Ave., Milwaukee, WI 53212. Call toll free: 1–800–669–4192. E-mail: RSBusiness@aol.com Visit the Web site: www.rethinkingschools.org.